OPENING CRED

A Word from the Editing Room... 2
Julian Sands.. 3
In Memoriam.. 4
Trails and Curses of a Comedy Icon - The '80s Pink Panther Films by Jonathon Dabell 5
'There Must Be Some Way Out of Here' - Withnail and I by Simon J. Ballard.. 11
Ms .45 by Darren Linder.. 16
007 and the Quest for the ATAC - For Your Eyes Only by Bryan C. Kuriawa.. 21
The Gospel According to Spinal Tap by John Harrison.................... 28
Honkytonk Man by David Flack.. 34
Fanny and Alexander by Dr. Andrew C. Webber...................... 38
Michelle Pfeiffer in the '80s by Michael Campochiaro.................. 42
Lewis Collins - The Macaroni Combat Years by Ian Talbot Taylor..... 53
The Beastmaster by Kevin Nickelson.................................... 59
Mark L. Lester Interview.. 63
Mark L. Lester in the '80s by David Michael Brown.................... 69
Midnight Run by Peter Sawford.. 76
Dead & Buried by Joe Secrett.. 81
Blind Fury: Quality Nonsense by James Lecky.......................... 84
The Dollmaker by Rachel Bellwoar...................................... 90
Return of the Jedi by James Aaron...................................... 94
Closing Credits.. 99

Contributors this issue: James Aaron, Simon J. Ballard, Rachel Bellwoar, David Michael Brown, Michael Campochiaro, Jonathon Dabell, David Flack, John Harrison, Bryan C. Kuriawa, James Lecky, Darren Linder, Kevin Nickelson, Peter Sawford, Joe Secrett, Aaron Stielstra, Ian Talbot Taylor, Dr Andrew C. Webber. Caricature artwork by Aaron Stielstra.

All articles, photographs and specially produced artwork remain copyright their respective author/photographer/artist. Opinions expressed herein are those of the individual.

Design and Layout: Dawn Dabell
Copy Editor: Jonathon Dabell

Most images in this magazine come from the private collection of Dawn and Jonathon Dabell, or the writer of the corresponding article. Those which do not are made available in an effort to advance understanding of cultural issues pertaining to academic research. We believe this constitutes 'fair use' of any such copyrighted material as provided for in Section 107 of the US Copyright Law. In accordance with Title U.S.C Section 107, this magazine is sold to those who have expressed a prior interest in receiving the included information for research, academic and educational purposes.

Printed globally by Amazon KDP

A Word from the Editing Room

Hello '80s movie lovers!

Welcome to Issue 3 of 'Cinema of the '80s'. We're delighted to offer another jam-packed edition, with articles on films as varied as *This Is Spinal Tap* (1984), *Dead and Buried* (1981), *Return of the Jedi* (1983), *Ms .45* (1981), *Fanny and Alexander* (1982) and much more. We also have some great overview features on the likes of the '80s Pink Panther films, Lewis Collins' trio of macaroni combat pictures, and the decade according to Michelle Pfeiffer. We're also thrilled to present an exclusive interview with director Mark L. Lester as well as an accompnaying overview of his '80s movies.

May we take this opportunity to extend a warm welcome to our newest writer Michael Campochiaro, who leaps in at the deep end with the cover article of the latest issue. An established writer and massive Michelle Pfeiffer fan, Michael is a great addition to our ever-expanding team and we're fortunate to have his services. His article can be found on page 42.

We were chatting amongst ourselves recently about the difference between the '70s and the '80s in cinematic terms. The prevailing style of filmmaking, what was hot vs what was not, is fascinating to think about. There certainly seemed to be a greater appetite for lightweight comedy as the '80s progressed. We've probably covered more films in that genre in the first three issues of the '80s mag than in all eight issues of our sister '70s mag. Yet there are still lots of dark, gritty, edgy '80s movies out there, as well as a real boom in family-friendly adventure fare and the rapid rise of sword and sorcery offerings. Oh, what a decade it was to be a movie lover!

Anyway, let us not waste another word. It's time to leap headlong into Issue 3. Until next time, happy reading!

Dawn and Jonathon Dabell

Julian Sands

Regular readers will know that page three of this magazine is usually dedicated to a big name who has passed away since our last issue. On this occasion, we have decided to pay tribute to the British actor Julian Sands, who, at the time of writing, remains unaccounted for after going missing while hiking the Mount Baldy trail in the Californian mountains.

Efforts to locate Sands remain ongoing but, after four months of fruitless searching by experienced search-and-resuce teams, hopes of a happy outcome are extremely remote.

Born in Otley, West Yorkshire in 1958, Sands came to prominence in the '80s, quickly becoming recognisable and well-respeted star in a number of noteworthy productions.

His '80s movies were:
Privates on Parade (1983)
Oxford Blues (1984)
The Killing Fields (1984)
After Darkness (1985)
The Doctor and the Devils (1985)
A Room witha View (1985)
Gothic (1986)
Siesta (1987)
Vibes (1988)
Wherever You Are... (1988)
Warlock (1989)
Manika, A Later Life (1989)
Tennessee Nights (1989)

He remained busy and active in the industry right up to the point of his disappearance. As we write, he has four titles that are either in post-production or awaiting a release date.

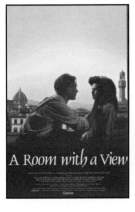

In Memoriam

**Robbie Coltrane
(1950-2022)**
Actor, known for *The Supergrass* (1985) and *Danny the Champion of the World* (1989).

**Ruggero Deodato
(1939-2022)**
Director, known for *Cannibal Holocaust* (1980) and *Phantom of Death* (1987).

**Melinda Dillon
(1939-2023)**
Actress, known for *A Christmas Story* (1983) and *Harry and the Hendersons* (1987).

**Andrés García
(1941-2023)**
Actor, known for *Carnada* (1980) and *Bordello* (1981).

**Hugh Hudson
(1936-2023)**
Director, known for *Chariots of Fire* (1981) and *Greystoke: The Legend of Tarzan, Lord of the Apes* (1984).

**Murray Melvin
(1932-2023)**
Actor, known for *Nutcracker* (1982) and *Little Dorrit* (1987).

**Edward R. Pressman
(1953-2023)**
Producer, known for *Conan the Barbarian* (1982) and *Wall Street* (1987).

**Tom Sizemore
(1961-2023)**
Actor, known for *Lock Up* (1989) and *Born on the Fourth of July* (1989).

**Stella Stevens
(1938-2023)**
Actress, known for *Wacko* (1982) and *Chained Heat* (1983).

**Topol
(1935-2023)**
Actor, known for *Flash Gordon* (1980) and *For Your Eyes Only* (1981).

TRAILS AND CURSES OF A COMEDY ICON

THE 80S PINK PANTHER FILMS

by Jonathon Dabell

The Pink Panther movies might have turned out differently if Peter Ustinov, the original casting choice for Inspector Clouseau, had not walked away from the role. Peter Sellers would become so synonymous with the character that nowadays it's hard to envisage Ustinov, or anyone else for that matter, playing him. Ustinov was lined up to play the bumbling detective in *The Pink Panther* (1963), alongside David Niven as the charming Raffles-type gentleman-thief Charles Lytton and Ava Gardner as Clouseau's beautiful but unfaithful wife Simone (who secretly fences Lytton's stolen goods). But the Mirisch Corporation, who were backing the film, refused to bow to Gardner's expensive, rather diva-ish demands for an entourage of personal staff, so she pulled out. Capucine was brought in to replace her. Ustinov, unhappy about the change of personnel, dropped out too.

As it turned out, a happy coincidence was just around the corner which would prove beneficial for all. While Gardner and Ustinov were relinquishing their roles in *The Pink Panther*, Peter Sellers was preparing to assume the role of small-time hustler Arthur Simon Simpson in Jules Dassin's heist movie *Topkapi*. But he'd become embroiled in constant disagreements with his co-star Maximilian Schell, who accused Sellers of being unreliable and unpredictable. It became clear one of them would need removing from the production if things were to progress smoothly. Ultimately it was Sellers who got his marching orders. Ustinov was brought in as his replacement and went on to win an Oscar for *Topkapi*. Meanwhile, the newly available Sellers was recruited to take the role of Inspector Clouseau in *The Pink Panther*.

Interestingly, Clouseau was not the main character in *The Pink Panther* but rather one of the supporting gallery, playing second fiddle to Niven's elegant lead. Others included Robert Wagner as Sir Charles' handsome young nephew, Claudia Cardinale as a Middle Eastern princess and Capucine as Clouseau's wife. Early in the shoot, director Blake Edwards noticed Sellers was stealing every scene he was in with his deadpan delivery, physical slapstick and earnest ineptitude, much of it semi-improvised. When the film came out, audiences lapped up Sellers' hilarious pratfalls and the film was a box-office hit. Despite Niven receiving top billing and giving a fine performance, it was Sellers who got most of the plaudits. In fact, several years later Niven was scheduled to walk onto the stage to present an Academy Award to the accompaniment of Henry Mancini's Pink Panther theme, but he requested a change of music because, as he pointed out: "You know, that really wasn't *my* film."

Clouseau would become the main character from the second film onwards. *A Shot in the Dark* (1964) was originally going to be a screen version of a stage play by Harry Kurnitz, with Anatole Litvak directing. But the production ran into trouble and Blake Edwards was asked to replace Litvak. Initially reluctant, he agreed to take over if the Mirisch Corporation permitted him to rewrite the lead character as Inspector Clouseau. He felt a mix of choreographed and improvised comedy would work well within the story, especially if the whole thing was presented as a second Clouseau outing. What emerged was perhaps the high-water mark of the series, an inspired whodunit full of mishaps, misunderstandings, sight gags,

5

verbal puns and ridiculous situations. It also set a template for subsequent entries to follow, introducing recurring characters and running jokes. Supporting characters destined to appear again and again as the series progressed included Inspector Dreyfus (Herbert Lom), Clouseau's manservant Kato (Burt Kwouk) and Dreyfus' assistant François (André Maranne).

By the time shooting ended on *A Shot in the Dark*, Edwards' relationship with Sellers had deteriorated to such an extent they vowed not to work together again. Within four years, they were back on good enough terms to put their differences aside to make *The Party* (1968). In the meantime, the Mirisch Corporation released a third film featuring Clouseau (*Inspector Clouseau* [1968]) without the participation of the regular cast and crew - Bud Yorkin took over directorial duties and the bumbling inspector was played by Alan Arkin, a fine actor but not a natural comedian. Sellers' career after *The Party* was littered with ill-advised roles in a run of poor films, almost all of them critical and commercial bombs. He was in the deepest doldrums by the time Edwards approached him about reviving the Clouseau character in 1974. It was a lifeline the struggling actor couldn't afford to ignore. He appeared in three Clouseau entries in the '70s, all commercially successful - *The Return of the Pink Panther* (1975), *The Pink Panther Strikes Again* (1976) and *Revenge of the Pink Panther* (1978).

Next up would have been an entry called *Romance of the Pink Panther*, which Sellers had written with the help of Jim Moloney (the scriptwriter of what would prove Sellers' final film during his lifetime, *The Fiendish Plot of Fu Manchu*). At the time, Sellers and Edwards were experiencing another rift in their relationship, so Moloney was set to be the replacement director on this seventh Pink Panther film. The plot would see Clouseau becoming smitten with a cat burglar nicknamed "The Frog" (to be played by Pamela Stephenson). It was scheduled for release in 1981, but pre-production was halted in its tracks when Sellers suffered a sudden fatal heart attack in July 1980. He was only 54 years old. It seemed certain the Pink Panther series was over without its iconic star, though the idea was briefly floated to carry on with Dudley Moore assuming the Clouseau role. Moore, riding the crest of a wave thanks to the success of *Arthur* (1981), was unwilling to commit to a long-running series of films and didn't fancy trying to win the favour of audiences who had grown to love Sellers in the role.

It was at this point that Blake Edwards came up with an idea which, on paper at least, looked viable. He had originally intended to release *The Pink Panther Strikes Again* as a three-hour comedy spectacle, a zany chase epic akin to his earlier *The Great Race* (1965). He'd shot acres of footage to this end, but United Artists expressed concern at the film's proposed length and instructed him

to cut it to a more digestible running time (the finished product ran at 103 minutes). With Sellers dead but most of the supporting actors still alive, Edwards came up with the idea of resurrecting the unused footage from *The Pink Panther Strikes Again* and splicing it into a new film. There wasn't enough usable footage to make a complete and coherent story, but there was enough to form the bones of a narrative. By shooting new material and adding it to the existing unused footage, Edwards felt he could piece together a seventh Pink Panther movie.

The result was *Trail of the Pink Panther* (1982) which starts with a brief pre-credits sequence in which a priceless gemstone, the 'Pink Panther Diamond', is stolen from a museum in the fictional Middle Eastern country of Lugash (referenced regularly throughout the series). We then launch into the customary animated credits sequences, a popular feature of all the Panther films, with an opening note dedicating the film "To Peter... the one and only Inspector Clouseau" while Henry Mancini's sublime main theme kicks in.

We first catch up with Clouseau (Sellers in archive footage) visiting his disguise maker "The Great Balls" (Harvey Korman). This entire sequence, excised from

Strikes Again, provokes initial confusion since Balls had appeared more recently in *Revenge of the Pink Panther* where he was portrayed by series regular Graham Stark. Soon after, Clouseau learns he has been called upon to find the missing diamond. He immediately suspects Sir Charles Lytton, aka the Phantom (David Niven), of being the thief. But Clouseau being the fool he is, he forgets Sir Charles now lives in the south of France and sets off for England to interrogate him. While on the plane, Edwards incorporates another unused sequence in which a heavily disguised Clouseau gets stuck in the cramped toilet. Similarly, when he arrives at the airport in London, we see Sellers interacting with Dudley Sutton, Leonard Rossiter and Colin Blakely in another scene removed from *Strikes Again*.

Viewers are treated to several more previously unused sequences featuring Sellers. But then, around the halfway point, Edwards runs out of old outtakes and is forced to shift the focus of the story. He accomplishes this by showing Clouseau on his way to Lugash to investigate the scene of the robbery, but the plane goes missing and is presumed lost during its flight to the Middle East.

At this point, ambitious TV journalist Marie Jouvet (Joanna Lumley) becomes the central character. She is determined to find out what has become of Clouseau and searches for clues by interviewing the people who knew him. The scenes of her speaking to his old friends and adversaries are newly shot, though flashbacks are sometimes incorporated making use of scenes from earlier films. When Marie speaks to Sir Charles Lytton, for example, there is a lengthy replay of a scene from *The Pink Panther* in which an elderly gentleman tries to cross the road in the dead of night but can't get to the other side because a manic car chase is taking place around him.

There is some confusion in continuity here because Sir Charles is shown to be happily married to Clouseau's ex-wife Simone (Capucine). They describe how they got together soon after the events depicted in *The Pink Panther* and have been madly in love ever since. Attentive viewers will remember that in *The Return of the Pink Panther*, Sir Charles was played by Christopher Plummer and had been happily married to a character called Lady Claudine Lytton (Catherine Schell) for many years. The reason for this apparent goof is unclear, though it might have something to do with ITC (the production company responsible for *The Return of the Pink Panther*) refusing to allow unused footage from that film to be used here. In some ways, it feels like the events of *Return* are ignored entirely in *Trail*.

Marie Jouvet's investigations also lead her to speak to the likes of Inspector Dreyfus, Kato and Hercule Lajoy (Clouseau's sidekick from *A Shot in the Dark*). A great scene involves Dreyfus being given the chance to eulogise Clouseau on television. He fights to stifle giggles while describing the missing man, but everyone watching assumes he is trying to keep his grief under control. A similar gag had been used in *Revenge of the Pink Panther* when Clouseau was lying low, pretending to be dead, and Dreyfus was called upon to give a heartfelt speech of condolence at his fake funeral.

Marie is kidnapped during the course of her investigation by the henchmen of gangster Bruno Langois (Robert Loggia... more confusion here, as the last time we saw Loggia in the series was in *Revenge of the Pink Panther* where he played the hood Al Marchione). Bruno doesn't want the nosey journalist to find Clouseau because his criminal empire has flourished since the "great" detective disappeared. Her final interviewee is Clouseau's father (Robert Mulligan), a clumsy eccentric who lives on a rural vineyard. He recounts stories of his son's childhood and early adult years as a soldier in the French Resistance, all characterised by typical mishaps and mayhem.

"The newest and funniest 'Panther' of them all" declared the theatrical poster of *Trail of the Pink Panther*. Audiences and (especially) critics didn't agree. The film was a flop and found itself on the receiving end of some pretty brutal reviews. "A necrophiliac excuse for a movie," derided one particularly unimpressed critic. It's hard to defend the story structure, which is very flimsy and feels like two incohesive halves. It also doesn't help that the previously unused footage is generally much funnier than the newly shot material. Lom and Mulligan have funny moments, but all the best jokes come from the archive. Once Clouseau exits the story, things definitely feel flatter... but there *are* good moments dotted about for fans of this brand of slapstick and silliness.

There was a sad footnote to all this which further damaged *Trail of the Pink Panther*'s financial prospects. Lynne Frederick, who had been married to Sellers at the time of his death, filed a lawsuit against the producers on the grounds that the film insulted the memory of her late husband. Further bolstering her claim was a written clause in which Sellers had forbidden the use of old, rejected outtakes at a later point. Since Edwards had wilfully ignored this agreement by resurrecting so much previously unseen material, the court ruled in favour of Frederick and she was awarded $1,475,000 in compensation.

One might have expected the Lynne Frederick lawsuit to put an end to any further Panther entries. But *Curse of the Pink Panther* (1983) had been shot simultaneously with *Trail* and didn't include any old outtakes, so its release went ahead as scheduled.

In this one, the authorities come up with the theory that the only way to find Clouseau is to assign a detective to the case who shares the missing man's resourcefulness and ingenuity. They use a database of the world's registered police officers to select the right man. But Dreyfus is desperate for Clouseau not to be found, so he reprogrammes the computer to select the most witless, clueless, inept policeman in the world to carry out the investigation.

The man chosen is Clifton Sleigh (Ted Wass), a dim-witted and accident-prone sergeant who works for the N.Y.P.D. Sleigh heads to France to take up the hunt for the missing Clouseau. Of course, only Dreyfus knows that Sleigh is incompetent, so everyone who is happier with Clouseau being missing is determined to keep it that way... which means Sleigh must die! Bruno Langois

(Loggia again) puts out a contract on the newly arrived American, and various other parties want to see him dead too. Sleigh makes his way around Europe, inadvertently surviving assassination attempts and uncovering clues by sheer dumb luck. He eventually locates Clouseau (we in the audience realise it, even if Sleigh doesn't) hiding in a villa in France with a new face.

At almost 2 hours, *Curse of the Pink Panther* is somewhat overlong. Wass tries hard and demonstrates some talent for physical comedy, but he lacks Sellers' natural gift for hilarity. The best moments belong to Lom (twitchily hilarious as ever as Dreyfus) and guest star Turk Thrust II as the plastic-surgery-enhanced Clouseau. Eagle-eyed viewers may remember there was a guest star billed as Turk Thrust in *A Shot in the Dark* (director Bryan Forbes used the pseudonym for his short but hilarious cameo as a guitar-strumming patron at a nudist colony). In *Curse of the Pink Panther*, Roger Moore is billed as Turk Thrust II for his extended cameo as Clouseau. The story leads us to believe that Clouseau himself stole the Pink Panther Diamond, having grown tired of being a policeman. He swiped the gem in order to retire to a life of anonymity and luxury. Moore sends himself up delightfully and manages to capture the immaculate timing and some of the mannerisms of Sellers. It's particularly impressive that he shot his scenes during a couple of days off from filming *Octopussy*, and nailed it without a rehearsal.

David Niven returns for the final film of his career. He was gravely ill during the shoot of *Trail* and *Curse* and was too weak to speak clearly (the voice we hear on the audio track is actually the impersonator Rich Little dubbing Niven's lines). He is joined by Capucine and Robert Wagner, back as Sir Charles' suave nephew. Wass' funniest moment occurs when he visits the three Lyttons at their villa. Detective Sleigh sits on an inflatable pool toy shaped like a duck, and as he settles into the seat the duck's head pops up between his legs suggesting an erect penis. A house-servant quickly removes the air valve, causing the duck's head to slowly go limp, provoking a sheepish look from Sleigh while the three Lyttons attempt to stifle smirks. Joanna Lumley appears too, but whereas she played the blonde-haired journalist Marie Jouvet in *Trail of the Pink Panther*, this time she is cast as Clouseau's raven-haired lover and accomplice Countess Chandra. The same actors playing different roles is something which happened a lot throughout the Pink Panther series - Robert Loggia, Peter Arne, Graham Stark, Douglas Wilmer and Claudia Cardinale being other stars who returned in different guises in later entries. Look quick too for Steve Franken in an early scene set in New York. His drunken playboy turns up in a limousine and propositions Sleigh, who is in drag at the time, disguised as a prostitute as part of a 'sting' operation. Franken's character, one Harvey Hamilcard III, is clearly modelled on Dudley Moore's Arthur - one wonders if this is a subtle in-joke referencing the recent unsuccessful attempt to persuade Moore to replace Sellers as Clouseau? Or maybe the role was originally intended as a cameo for 'Cuddly' Dudley?

The plan was to launch a new series of Pink Panther movies with Clifton Sleigh as the main character. Alas, *Curse of the Pink Panther* performed disappointingly at the box office and future productions were cancelled. It wasn't until the belated *Son of the Pink Panther* (1993) - in which Roberto Benigni played Jacques Gambrelli (Clouseau's illegitimate son with Elsa Gambrelli from *A Shot in the Dark*) - that

another Panther movie was seen. It failed to ignite much interest among audiences and was largely panned by critics, bringing to an end the original cycle of films. Steve Martin would assume the Clouseau role for a 21st century reboot.

Trail of the Pink Panther and *Curse of the Pink Panther* are generally unloved among the Pink Panther canon. The general consensus is that Blake Edwards flew against common sense and good taste by trying to keep the series alive after Sellers' death. There's some truth in that, but it's unfair to say the films lack laughs and enjoyable moments. They are certainly not as wretched as their critical reputation suggests. Yes, the entries made during Sellers' lifetime were better, but the '80s duo have their moments and deserve to be seen.

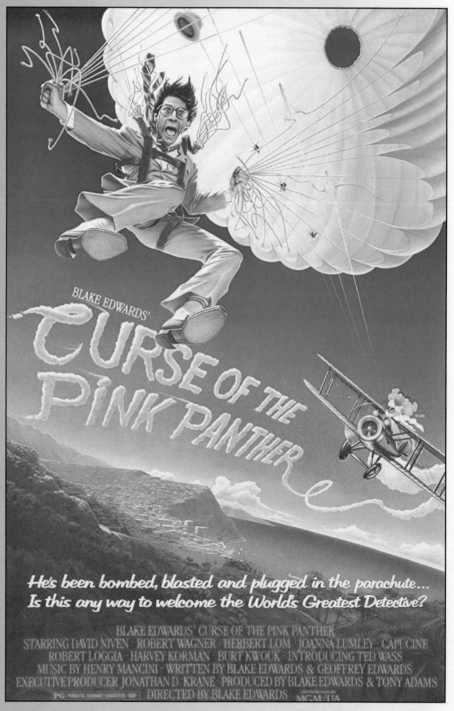

WITHNAIL AND I

by Simon J. Ballard

Good ol' George Harrison. As well as being a member of that popular beat combo from Liverpool, he co-founded production company HandMade Films with his business partner Denis O'Brien to help finance *Monty Python's Life of Brian* in 1979 because he really wanted to see it come to fruition. He later joked it was the most expensive cinema ticket in movie history!

Seven years later, former youthful actor Bruce Robinson got to turn his unpublished, semi-autobiographical novel 'Withnail & I' into a film of the same name backed by HandMade. As a small, independent company, HandMade offered Robinson the chance to turn his less-than-conventional script into a finished product without corporate interference.

As a recovering alcoholic who once spent the night in a bin, I find myself able to identify with the poverty-stricken dipsomaniacs Withnail and Marwood (the "I" of the title) as they limp across the fag-end of the '60s, wasting their days in a squalid flat in Camden and waiting oh-so-helplessly for the next acting job to materialise. When I was out of work for a period, I used to wake up in the morning and proceed to drink myself into oblivion, often - ironically - watching this very film whilst doing so.

In attempting to sum up the plot, many fans of *Withnail and I* inadvertently make it sound like one the dullest films ever. "So, these friends, right? They're out-of-work actors, they go away for a holiday and it goes badly, and... well, that's it." To describe *Withnail & I* thus misses the core hilarity and wistful beauty of the movie; the oh-so-quotable dialogue, the self-destructive yet co-dependent friendship between the two protagonists, the sparklingly caustic chemistry between Richard E. Grant and Paul McGann.

Withnail is self-obsessed and believes every single casting director is a fool not to recognise his immense talent as an actor. He is bitter, misanthropic and only stops drinking when his benefits run out. The character was based on Vivian MacKerrell, an actor friend of Robinson's with whom he shared digs in the '60s. He was described by Robinson as a Jack of all trades yet master of none. MacKerrell was quite handsome in his prime (which didn't last long thanks to his excessive drinking), and one of his few acting roles was, rather aptly, in a BBC *Play for Today* instalment called *Edna, the Inebriate Woman* (1971). He was also in Stephen Weeks' *Ghost Story* (not the Peter Straub one) in 1974, and... well, not much else. His heavy drinking scuppered his career, and, after contracting throat cancer, he continued to consume booze by injecting alcohol directly into his stomach. He was 50 when he died, which is rather sobering.

How subversive, then, to hire Richard E. Grant, a man in real life allergic to alcohol, to bring MacKerrell's alter-ego Withnail to life. Despite this aversion, Robinson made the relatively unknown Grant, here making his cinematic debut, drink vast quantities of booze to gain the "chemical memory" of a drunkard. Suffice to say, Grant threw up after each drink.

What convinced Robinson that Grant was the man for Withnail was his audition, during which he performed the kitchen scene in which the two young layabouts believe something may be alive in the sink - a rat, possibly. Grant shrieking the line "Fork it!" was the clincher, after claiming that "...the entire sink's gone rotten."

Before I sobered up in 2020, I was drinking neat vodka daily and I can say, with ashamed experience, that Grant's portrayal of a perpetual drinker is spot on. He slurs without going too overboard, he staggers without descending into exaggeration, he manages to capture to perfection the behaviour of a piss-artist who is functioning (just) as a waking human.

McGann had already made a strong impression in 1986, appearing on television in Alan Bleasdale's WWI-set drama *The Monocled Mutineer*. His character Marwood, unnamed in the film (though you can just about discern his name on a telegram he receives whilst staying at Crow Crag), is a perfect foil to the narcissistic nihilism of Withnail. He reads and writes poetry and is more philosophical about their rather rancid resting period. He can also match Withnail in the drinking stakes, meaning there is no leverage

on their behaviour, no-one to admonish or reproach. He is the screen representation of Robinson, who tended to nurse-maid MacKerrell during his frequent flights of fantasy.

Specifically, it was from his time as an actor that Robinson drew inspiration for Marwood's predicament concerning the unwanted attention of Withnail's rotund and fruity Uncle Monty, played here fabulously by Richard Griffiths, more interested in firm young carrots than growing flowers. It is from him that they procure the rusting key to his shambolic cottage (how suitable!) in the wilds of the Lake District, just outside Penrith.

Italian director Franco Zeffirelli essentially enforced his not-so-delicate attentions on the young and rather dreamy-looking Robinson in 1968 on the set of *Romeo and Juliet* while the young actor was playing Benvolio. Uncle Monty advancing on Marwood wearing an open dressing gown and make-up can be viewed as Robinson attempting to ridicule and shame Zeffirelli for his actions.

Just when everything seemed to be in place for filming to get underway, two obstacles threatened to derail proceedings. Firstly, in rehearsals, Robinson became troubled by McGann's strong Liverpudlian accent and promptly fired him. He relented when McGann promised he could deliver a decent Home Counties enunciation. Secondly, Denis O'Brien, mindful of the budget and the need to reap it back at the box office, contemplated shutting down the entire production on the first day of filming. The performances of the leads just weren't what he considered proper comedy acting, and he was worried the script wasn't conventionally comedic enough. He feared they were embarking on a film that had no chance of finding an audience. It is undoubtedly hard to describe - there are no gags as such, just an endless stream of idiosyncratic lines.

The film opens with a version of *A Whiter Shade of Pale* performed by King Curtis & the Kingpins. Robinson felt that Procol Harum's own recording, an archetypal '60s song, was too clichéd. The camera crawls around the flat shared by Withnail and Marwood, the latter making coffee in a kitchen that is a cesspit of dirty crockery, milk bottles growing a strain of furry mould that may well be a cure for something, and half-eaten unidentifiable foodstuffs everywhere. You can almost smell it. Marwood ladles his coffee with a spoon from a bowl rather than drinking from one of the cups, for obvious reasons.

There are those who would criticise the decision to litter this hellhole of a flat with antique furniture, such as the wooden cabinet full of plates and a splendid clock on the mantlepiece, but Robinson pointed out that during the period in which *Withnail & I* is set, such items could be picked up for shillings from the market.

High praise should be given to production designer Michael Pickwoad who, in later life, designed the second Tardis interior for Matt Smith's Doctor Who, That's not the only connection to *Doctor Who*, of course. My first viewing of *Withnail and I*, which took place in 1996, was inspired by the fact McGann had just been cast as the Time Lord for a one-off TV-movie. Griffiths was also once considered to play the Doctor in the '80s, and Grant did play a version of the Ninth Doctor in an animated special called *Scream of the Shalka* (2003). Interestingly, Grant's Doctor's costume was a high-wing collar with cravat and rather long overcoat, a more elegant version of the shabby dress clinging to Withnail. Oh, and the drunk former General turned publican who runs the Penrith pub The Crow is portrayed by Noel Johnson, who appeared twice in *Doctor Who* - firstly in the Patrick Troughton serial *The Underwater Menace* (1967) and later in the Jon Pertwee caper *Invasion of the Dinosaurs* (1974).

It is inside the flat we get one of two wonderful unscripted moments from Grant. Having rubbed embrocation all over his body to keep warm, naturally proclaiming there is nothing left in the tube for Marwood, Withnail demands to have some booze and is forced to resort to the only liquid they have left - lighter fluid! Pouring what he thought was water into his mouth, Grant was visibly shocked to

discover Robinson had filled the container with vinegar! The other occasion occurs later in the charmingly quaint Penrith Tea Rooms. Both pissed as farts, the duo declare it wise to "eat some cake, soak up the booze", and as Withnail threatens to return and install a jukebox to "liven up all you stiffs", Grant's laughter was not intended.

Before we reach the fresh air of Penrith, though, we must just hang around the flat and meet Danny (Ralph Brown), a purveyor of rare herbs and prescribed chemicals. The drug-dealer was based on two people, one of whom was a genuine dealer who later changed 'career' and became a stockbroker! Danny's languid, spaced-out voice was based on a hairdresser Robinson knew, and Brown got the part after travelling to Pinewood Studios wearing purple nail varnish and a wig, which impressed Robinson no end. Danny is a great character, who could easily have been over-played in lesser hands given his extraordinary nature, not to mention his kit which includes a 'voodoo doll' called the Emabalmer whose head contains pills, and a device that enables a drunken driver to be released from police custody without charge.

As the pair depart London, to the tune of Jimi Hendrix's *All Along the Watchtower*, we see a literal and figurative demolition taking place as the end of the decade fast approaches. The old brick tenements seen falling down were situated in Notting Hill, and were no doubt replaced with something dull and concrete as the dirtily stained

'70s reared up and gulped down good taste. The shot of Marwood staring out of the window of their battered Mark II Jag and flipping his shades down over his glasses is way cool, though!

In Cumbria, not far from Penrith, the derelict Sleddale Hall stands in for Monty's abode Crow Crag, owned at the time by North West Water. Pickwoad decorated the interior with a fine eye for detail. In the shot where Withnail sits dejectedly to "enjoy his holiday", notice the cobweb-bestrewn range, the portraits of King George and Queen Mary either side of it speaking of Monty's patriotism and private school upbringing, and the peeling walls and dust-coated table in the middle of the room speaking of neglect.

Believe it or not, the shots as they enter the house at dead of night with the rain pouring outside were actually filmed during a hot summer's day, with blackout sheets keeping the sunlight at bay. It was in fact the first scene to be filmed, and was another cause for concern from O'Brien who feared Robinson planned to shoot the whole production so darkly.

When Uncle Monty arrives, a marvellously subtle transformation takes place. The cottage suddenly sports net curtains, the walls are a pinker shade of pink and candles burn from golden candelabras. He may insinuate he would like to 'enter' Marwood by means of burglary, but otherwise he does bring a touch of class to the place!

During the cottage scenes, a note of melancholy enters the frame. Monty is a tragic figure, a gay man who has spent his life in the shadows, hidden away in public lavatories. When Marwood pushes away his advances by pretending to be in love with Withnail, and claims the latter is afraid to openly show his homosexuality, Monty is heartbroken for them.

It is also whilst on holiday that a telegram arrives with an offer of work for Marwood. Withnail is distraught. Jealousy? Oh yes. But more importantly, he realises their friendship is about to fragment. Maybe he really was in love with Marwood, or just cannot

contemplate a life without him. His Hamlet soliloquy when Marwood departs declares: "Man delights not me: no, nor women neither", so perhaps his sexuality is open to fluidity? Had Robinson shot the climax from his novel, Withnail would have poured wine into the rifle belonging to Monty and fired both barrels into his mouth. The film more-or-less declares he will commit suicide in slow motion, drinking forever alone. It is for this reason that *Withnail & I* is an excellent film; for the underlying tragedy that runs through the side-splitting dialogue, for reflecting life in unflinching detail. Robinson wrote what he knew, and through this writing we sense real truth.

HandMade Films Presents

WITHNAIL and I

"WITHNAIL and I"
A PAUL HELLER Production
PAUL McGANN   RICHARD E. GRANT   RICHARD GRIFFITHS
Music by DAVID DUNDAS *and* RICK WENTWORTH
Photographed by PETER HANNAN
Co-Produced by DAVID WIMBURY
Executive Producers GEORGE HARRISON *and* DENIS O'BRIEN
Produced by PAUL HELLER
Written and Directed by BRUCE ROBINSON

Ms .45

by Darren Linder

1981 was such an absolute pinnacle of cinema that an entire article, or even a magazine, could be devoted to just this fact. There were numerous groundbreaking landmark movies in the horror/thriller genre from that year. The Gods ordered an international shake and bake of creativity, gore and unique violence for 1981 that hasn't been equaled since. A short list of stellar horror films from the year would include *Halloween II, The Howling, The Evil Dead, The Prowler, An American Werewolf in London, Possession, Scanners* and *The Burning*. Italian horror director Lucio Fulci squeezed in two films in the same year, *The Beyond* and The *House by the Cemetery*. The list continues with non-horror greats like *Escape from New York, Thief, Nighthawks, The Road Warrior, Das Boot, Outland, Dragonslayer* and *Raiders of the Lost Ark*.

New York City director Abel Ferrara released what I consider to be one of his best films in 1981 as well, the disturbing rape-revenge movie *Ms .45*. Ferrara took the fledgling vigilante subgenre, which arguably began with the 1974 Charles Bronson film *Death Wish*, and made it more personal and poetic by having the woman herself getting the revenge. Of course, we shouldn't forget the likes of the 1973 Swedish film *Thriller: A Cruel Picture* (aka *They Call Her One Eye*) and *I Spit on Your Grave* from 1978. Wes Craven's early *The Last House on the Left*, released in 1972, also dealt with this topic. But Ferrara's offering may be the

first rape-revenge film of the '80s. It's as if Ferrara took VHS tapes of *Taxi Driver, Death Wish* and *They Call Her One Eye* and put them in a blender with blood, lipstick and a sprinkling of feminism.

A Manhattan seamstress named Thana (Zoe Lund) is raped twice in the same day on her way home from work; first in an alley and then again in her own apartment. She overpowers and kills the second rapist and acquires his gun. She then uses this .45 pistol to murder various men around NYC. Lund was only 17 years old when this film was made. Similar to Bronson in *Death Wish*, she doesn't go after her two specific rapists; she just goes after men in general. She targets a sleazy and predatory photographer, a pimp beating up a call girl and an Arab sheik who tries to solicit her for sex. These are indeed bad men who deserve some sort of retribution, but certainly not death. It's a PTSD-fueled overreaction of psychosis and wish fulfillment fantasy. I won't claim that this exploitation film is any kind of feminist manifesto, but it's far deeper than one would expect, with lots of interesting symbolism and unique details.

I've always viewed *Death Wish* as a drama, not an action piece. People confuse the original film with the four sequels, which become more cartoonish as they go. The first film is a character study of a man who has a mental breakdown after the rape of his wife and daughter which leaves the former dead and the latter catatonic. He goes around New York City presenting himself as a victim who then kills the muggers who inevitably attack him. Some have called *Ms .45* a 'female *Death Wish*.' There are similarities for sure. Both lead characters present themselves as meek victims to encourage criminals, and both return home after their first kill to throw up. But in Ferrara's film, the vigilante is killing people who just have the *potential* for evil, but in most cases haven't attempted any harm or crimes. Thana is killing these men for what they represent; for their mere potential for violence and rape. In the climactic party scene (which I'll talk about more later), we overhear conversations from some of the men that allude to them being bad guys. Pre-emptive revenge isn't usually a tenet of vigilantism like it is here, even though it is rewarding to live vicariously through Thana as she blasts her way through the douchebags of New York City.

Over the course of the film, her presentation/fashion changes. She starts the film dressing very conservatively, blending in, seeming bookish and plain. As she embraces her persona, she starts dressing to attract the attention of men, so that she can find the bad ones and execute them. She wears more red and black. She starts applying dramatic makeup. She wears black leather pants and stylish hats or hoods, evoking memories of Little Red Riding Hood.

In an interesting bit of casting trivia, director Ferrara himself plays the first rapist. He wears a disturbing mask and threatens Thana with a pistol before raping her in an alley over a garbage can. There is then a God's-eye overhead view of Thana lying on the concrete with the dumpsters, as she is now discarded garbage (to the rapist). Might this be a commentary on how male directors figuratively rape, exploit and obsess on their lead actresses? How the starlets are used and then thrown away? Or was it just a money-saving measure in a low budget movie to have the director play a small role? I would love to ask Abel about the reasons he cast himself in this film.

When Thana overcomes the second rapist in her apartment, she grabs a nearby glass paperweight and smashes him in the head with it. The paperweight is a red apple, obviously evoking the Christian mythology of Eve taking the bite of the apple and then being blamed for original sin. She turns the tables on this idea of forbidden fruit and being punished by God for being guilty of this purported sin. Then, when she finishes off the rapist, she grabs an iron off the ironing board and crushes his head in. It's fitting that an iron is used as the weapon here. Not only is it a common tool in her profession, but it is also the symbol of '50s prescribed gender stereotypes of American housewives handling the chores of domesticity.

After she kills the rapist in her apartment, she then has to figure out how to dispose of the body. These scenes reminded me of the dark humor of various Hitchcock

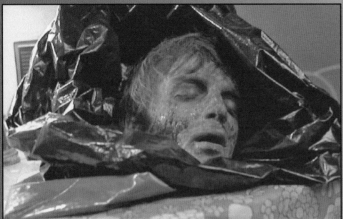

films, although definitely R-rated. Thana cuts up the body in her bathtub, wraps up the pieces in garbage bags, then disposes of them in unique ways. She places one in the chopping cart of a mentally ill homeless woman. She dumps some in a sidewalk garbage can, later humorously discovered by another homeless man. She tries grinding up the meat and mixing it in with her dog's food. She drops a bag in the trunk of the car of a distracted man packing to leave. From his license plate we see that he is likely driving back to Georgia. In a further direct homage to Hitchcock, there is a scene of a close-up of water spiraling into the bathtub drain dissolving into a shot of a character's eye. This is, of course, one of the most famous shots in the classic *Psycho*.

In one scene Thana goes walking around Central Park at night, exactly like Charles Bronson did in *Death Wish*. She becomes surrounded by five men who clearly plan to rape, beat and mug her. She draws her gun and shoots them all, executing the only one still alive after the initial shots. Dealing with enemies that are around rapidly and precisely shows her growing confidence and skill. This scene has to be homage to the scene in *Death Wish*, and if they had used the exact same staircase in *Ms .45* it would have been even more apparent. The scene where Bronson spins around to shoot an assailant coming up behind him was so iconic that they used it on most of the posters and promotions for the film.

One of the more unusual and interesting scenes is where Thana is in a bar with a man who seems to be telling her his life story about his last relationship. Since Thana is mute, the man is just talking endlessly. He doesn't even notice or care that she isn't replying verbally at all, he's essentially speechifying. Once his story reveals that he is a bit unhinged and has a violent side (he admits to murdering his ex's cat), she decides he will be her next victim. The fact that this man doesn't think it strange that Thana never speaks may imply that some men do not want an actual conversation with a woman, they just want to talk at her. No interruptions, no clarifying questions, no reflections, not even any nodding or verbal prompts. Just listening to his monologue. To some men, this would be the perfect woman. But to this man, she will be his death.

I also appreciated that this film does not fall into the typical tropes of sexualizing the main character under the male gaze. Films like *Death Wish II*, *Savage Streets* and *Thriller: A Cruel Picture* are relentless in the use of nudity and sexual violence. Thana is never seen naked, which is unusual for a film about rape. In fact, there is no nudity at all in this movie. Contrast this with Ferrara's very next film *Fear City* (1984), where there are truckloads of nudity from Melanie Griffith and Rae Dawn Chong. But in *Ms .45* the camera does not objectify Thana like so many other films in the genre do. There are no slow-motion shots of her gearing up for the night, no gratuitous shots of

her cleavage or her legs in high heels, and no shots of her stroking her gun like a phallus. There are numerous scenes that show her suffering the PTSD side effects of a traumatic violent rape. The film is shot in an almost neutral or flat way, likely by design. In fact, it wouldn't surprise me at all if it were revealed that a woman, or Zoe Lund herself, secretly directed this film. Her character is empowering and confident, instead of being a meek victim in a salacious exploitation midnight movie.

One of my favorite scenes is when Thana is alone in her room getting ready for the Halloween party. We see her for the first time in her costume, that of a nun with a large rosary necklace and garish red lipstick. She kisses each bullet with reverence as she loads her .45, as if blessing them. She is a priestess of death and this is her sacrament. Then she lifts the gun and begins pantomiming shooting people. She looks at herself in the mirror and blows kisses in between her fake gunshots. Distorted sound effects of echoing gunshots are added to the soundtrack in a surreal touch that makes the scene especially memorable. She looks around furtively and it almost feels like this was rehearsal footage. She is feral and animalistic. It is a direct homage or reflection of the infamous scene in Martin Scorsese's *Taxi Driver* where Travis Bickle is talking to himself in the mirror, imagining what the final violent confrontation might start like. Even if you haven't seen *Taxi Driver*, the "You talkin' to me?" scene is a universally known pop-culture reference. Also, the image of a nun brandishing a handgun is a delicious blasphemy. Thana points the gun right at herself in the mirror, touching the tip of the gun to its reflection. She has accepted that she may destroy herself in the upcoming slaughter, and much like Travis Bickle, she does not care.

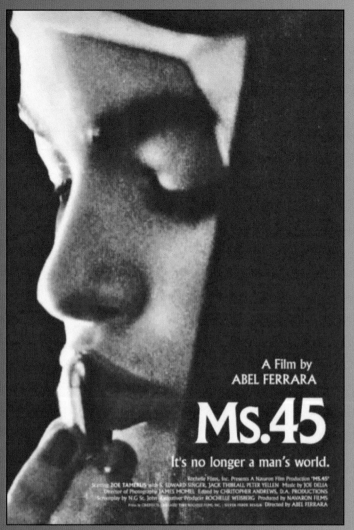

A Film by
ABEL FERRARA

Ms.45

It's no longer a man's world.

Rochelle Films, Inc. Presents A Navaron Film Production "MS.45"
Starring ZOE TAMERLIS with S. EDWARD SINGER, JACK THIBEALL, PETER YELLEN · Music by JOE DELIA
Director of Photography JAMES MOMEL · Edited by CHRISTOPHER ANDREWS, D.A. PRODUCTIONS
Screenplay by N.G St. John · Executive Producer ROCHELLE WEISBERG · Produced by NAVARON FILMS
Directed by ABEL FERRARA

The Halloween party is the climax of the film, and it compares with *Carrie* for bleak conclusions where a fun social event with dancing ends in many horrific deaths. Thana's nun costume is perfect, especially with all the previous religious imagery. Director Ferrara was raised Catholic, so having his female killer dressed as a nun must have been a meaningful juxtaposition for him personally. Another title for the film was *Angel of Vengeance,* and even her name, Thana, is an allusion to Thanatos, the Greek god of death. Once she starts murdering people at this party, the entire sequence is shown in slow motion. It's a Sam Peckinpah style slo-mo slaughter complete with realistic blood squibs flying right at the camera. They even slow down the audio effects, which makes the cries and screams sound like the growling of animals. At this slow speed, the existing lights pulse and flicker as she moves through the crowd like the angel of death. Halloween decorations of a spider's web cover the wall behind her, fitting as she has been setting traps and luring men to her. Seeing people dressed as demons and monsters running away from a real-life grim reaper in slow motion is the surreal highlight of the film for me.

Thana only targets the men in the room, but we are given some slight backstory to some of them to illustrate that they too are bad guys. One talks about taking a vacation where he rented young virgin girls for sex, and another talks about going back on his promise to get a vasectomy and then getting his girlfriend pregnant. Other men in the party are just killed for being men. One interesting death is of a man wearing a wedding dress and wearing makeup. Thana hesitates just for a second before shooting him. His wig is pulled off as he falls and it is confirmed that he was indeed male. Potential spoilers ahead: The only person to stop panicking and act during this shooting is a woman, one of Thana's work friends. She grabs a large knife from the cake and holds it in front of her crotch, like a penis. In a film full of phallic imagery and gun worship, it's very interesting to see a woman brandishing the weapon that will penetrate Thana and stop the slaughter. Thana then utters her first and only word in the entire film: "Sister…"

Ms .45 is a great film worthy of reconsideration and appreciation. I consider it Ferrara's greatest work, right alongside *King of New York* and *Bad Lieutenant.* It is now finally available on Blu-ray, though watching it on VHS tape while eating popcorn might feel more apropos.

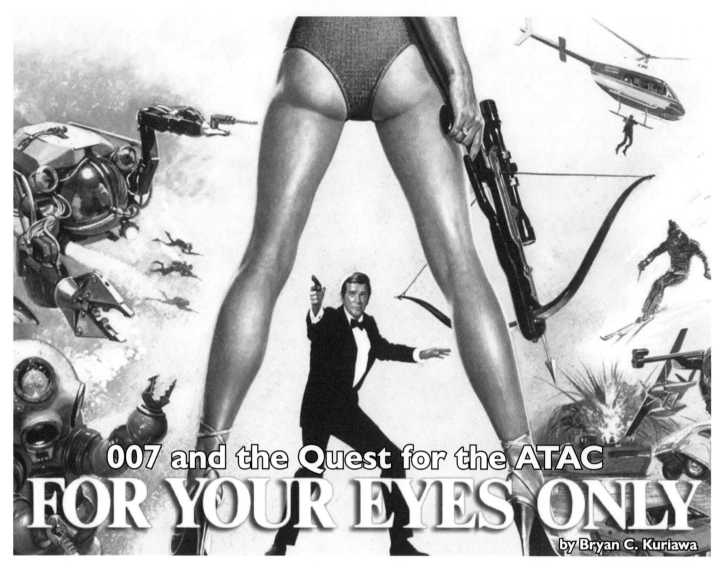

007 and the Quest for the ATAC
FOR YOUR EYES ONLY
by Bryan C. Kuriawa

By 1981, the James Bond series had been the biggest global film franchise for almost 20 years. Bolstering its durability during this period was the third official actor to play 007, Roger Moore.

Moore's first entry *Live and Let Die* (1973) had been a box-office smash, with audiences warming to his lighter interpretation of the character. But a lackluster second outing, *The Man with the Golden Gun* (1974), meant the series was at risk of entering a lull. Luckily Lewis Gilbert - who'd helmed *You Only Live Twice* (1967) - directed two commercial hits in a row, *The Spy Who Loved Me* (1977) and *Moonraker* (1979), to revive the series' fortunes.

Although *Moonraker* was popular with audiences, producer Albert R. Broccoli felt they'd gone too far by having Bond travel to outer space to fight a megalomaniacal billionaire intent on world destruction. He figured it was time to tone things down for the next adventure. EON felt the franchise needed to reposition itself towards a standard espionage storyline. Moore was brought back to continue his established, humorous take on the British superspy, but the latest entry would be characterized by a darker plot and style. The resulting film, *For Your Eyes Only* (1981), boasted a colorful supporting cast, a former

editor/assistant director (John Glen) taking his first steps into becoming a fully-fledged filmmaker, and a screenplay by series veterans Michael G. Wilson and Richard Maibaum.

"Before Setting Off on Revenge, You First Dig Two Graves"

In the Ionian Sea off Greece, the British spy vessel *St. Georges* is patrolling. While Greek fishermen work on deck, officers go about their duties below. On board is an advanced control system called ATAC which communicates with the British nuclear submarine fleet. When the fisherman accidently pull up a sea mine, the *St. Georges* is severely damaged and the crew is unable to activate the ATAC's self-destruct mechanism before she sinks.

Fearing the device could end up in Russian hands, the British government requests the services of oceanic archaeologist Sir Timothy Havelock (Jack Headley) to recover it. Before he can get started, Havelock and his wife are killed by a Cuban hitman, Hector Gonzalez (Stefan Kalipha). This is witnessed by the Havelocks' daughter Melina (Carole Bouquet).

Back in London, with M on leave, Bill Tanner (James

Villiers) sends James Bond (Moore) to locate Gonzalez at his residence in Spain. While monitoring Gonzalez, Bond witnesses him receiving money from an unknown figure with glasses (Michael Gothard). Bond is captured but, while being led away, Gonzalez is shot and killed by an arrow from a crossbow. In the ensuing mayhem Bond flees, but not before running into Gonzalez's crossbow-wielding assassin, who turns out to be Melina.

After his Lotus Esprit Turbo explodes, Bond and Melina have to make their escape from Gonzalez's men in a rickety Citroen 2CV. Returning to London, Bond identifies the man with glasses as an assassin named Locque. His next stop is the Italian ski resort of Cortina where he meets Greek businessman Kristatos (Julian Glover) who claims to have information about various parties interested in acquiring the ATAC. Among them are Russian agents and a smuggler named Columbo (Topol). It's up to 007 to prevent the ATAC falling into enemy hands which, if it happens, will endanger Britain's entire nuclear submarine fleet.

The directorial debut of Glen, *For Your Eyes Only* is an underrated gem in the series. With a strong cast and more realistic spy story, it marks an interesting detour for the long-running franchise.

"New Director, New Possibilities"

John Glen seemed a natural choice to helm the 12th 007 film. He'd previously worked as an assistant editor and sound editor on various film and television productions. His directorial entrance into the world of James Bond came at the best possible moment. Between 1968 and '69, he'd worked as second-unit director and editor on the sixth instalment *On Her Majesty's Secret Service*, which went on to be regarded as one of the most acclaimed of them all. On that film, Glen was taken under the wing of editor-turned-director Peter Hunt, and ended up working with him on further films including *Gold* (1974) and *Shout at the Devil* (1976). After falling out with Hunt while shooting the latter, Glen found himself returning to the orbit of 007.

Although Ernest Day was the official second-unit director on *The Spy Who Loved Me*, it was Glen who found himself assigned with the daunting task of filming a pivotal piece of footage for the pre-credits sequence. The sequence required stuntman Rick Sylvester, who'd performed a similar stunt for a Canadian whiskey ad in 'Playboy', to ski off the edge of a mountainside, freefall for several seconds, then open a Union Jack parachute seconds before hitting the ground. As audacious stunts go, it was very grand in scale. Filming the sequence at Baffin Island was hindered by poor weather and visibility which caused delays. Despite the anxiety of everyone involved, Glen persisted. Multiple cameras were set up to capture the stunt, but only one caught Sylvester's extraordinary ski fall as it happened. Glen was delighted when director Gilbert congratulated him on the amazing footage he'd captured. This pre-credits sequence is justly celebrated and remains one of the landmark moments in the series.

A massive box-office and critical success, *The Spy Who Loved Me* saved the James Bond franchise. Glen's services would be requested again for the sci-fi-laden *Moonraker*, which opened with a pre-credits sequence featuring a skydiving stunt. A specially designed head-camera, which a cameraman could wear without risk, was used to captured stuntmen B.J. Worth and Jake Lombard performing the dive. They did 88 jumps altogether to get the required footage. It was an epic sequence which marked a fantastic start to an unfairly maligned Bond outing.

Moonraker was another box-office success, but the sci-fi and fantasy elements attracted their share of criticism. As pre-production began on the next entry, the staff felt returning to a Fleming-esque approach was essential. While working on *The Sea Wolves* (1980), Glen was invited to lunch with Albert Broccoli, his wife Dana, stepson Michael G. Wilson, production designer Peter Lamont and effects director Derek Meddings. During their lunch, they discussed who would direct the next Bond film.

During a second lunch a few days later, Broccoli asked Glen if he would be interested in taking the reins. Glen accepted at once, describing that day as feeling like he was "walking on air." With a cool $28 million budget, Glen

had his money and production team in place, and all that remained was for him to yell "Action!"

"I'll Buy You a Delicatessen in Stainless Steel!"

Now on his fifth outing as Bond, Moore retains the onscreen persona he'd cultivated over the preceding years. He always played the part with a comedic sense of timing, a wit, lightness of tone and personality that were well-suited to the 007 productions being made at that time. In *For Your Eyes Only*, his interpretation remained as before albeit with minor tweaks.

His Bond takes a slightly parental role towards his love-interest Melina, worried that her quest for revenge may darken her future pursuits. At the same time, he tries to avoid the advances of a young figure-skater, Bibi (Lynn-Holly Johnson), who seems infatuated with him. We also see a darker side to his Bond, especially in a scene where he pursues Locque and eventually traps him in his car as it teeters on the side of a cliff. With the villain at his mercy, Bond kicks the car over the side and watches it plunge, with Locque still inside, onto the rocks far below. Moore struggled with the cold-blooded violence of this scene and originally wanted the pin he throws into the car to be what caused it to fall. Luckily, Glen was able to convince him to do the scene as intended.

As the vengeful half-British/half-Greek Melina, Bouquet makes an enigmatic Bond girl. Her voice has a slightly

monotone quality, but she makes up for it with an intense and striking face. Idolizing her father and wanting to continue his archeological explorations, Melina is hell-bent on revenge despite Bond's persistent warnings. Bouquet had made her splash in Luis Buñuel's *That Obscure Object of Desire* (1977) and had tried, unsuccessfully, to land the role of Holly Goodhead in *Moonraker*. After securing the part of Melina, she knew it wasn't Shakespeare level but didn't want to be "just another Bond girl." She also sparked the ire of the producers by claiming Moore was old enough to be her father. In subsequent years, Bouquet enjoyed a distinguished career in French and European productions, winning a Cesar as Best Actress for *Too Beautiful for You* (1989). Her most prominent later roles were in the anthology film *New York Stories* (1989) and the 2014 mini-series *Rosemary's Baby*.

As Kristatos, Julian Glover gives an understated performance, far removed from the cartoonish megalomaniacs exemplified by Blofeld, Hugo Drax, Elliot Carver or Gustav Graves. A prominent businessman with nefarious ties, he initially presents a friendly yet duplicitous façade. He tries to fool Bond into believing his foe is Milos Columbo, a former Greek resistance fighter with whom Kristatos fought against German occupation and, later, communist forces. Unlike most Bond villains, Kristatos' tone is one of building intensity - he never quite blows his top and is certainly no cackling madman. But he is savage minded, and his sadistic streak comes to the fore when he captures Bond and Melina and tries to dispose of them in an elaborately nasty way.

The best of the supporting cast is Topol as Columbo, one of the most enjoyable onscreen Bond allies. Initially presented as a villain, he turns out to be a pistachio-loving rogue who reveals Kristatos' deception. Charming and sociable, he could almost be a Greek version of 007. Born in British Palestine, Topol gained success in Israeli films during the '60s until his international breakout as Tevye in *Fiddler on The Roof* (1971), a role he'd portrayed on stage for several years prior to the movie version (and which he would return to after). His other major cinematic roles include the title character in Joseph Losey's *Galileo* (1975) and Hans Zarkov in the cult classic *Flash Gordon* (1980).

Of the remaining performers, Lynn-Holly Johnson is delightful as the infatuated Bibi. In one scene, she parades around in nothing but a towel in Bond's hotel room, but he resists her advances by suggesting she should get dressed so he can buy her an ice cream! Desmond Llewelyn and Lois Maxwell do well too, in brief roles as Q and Moneypenny respectively.

On an interesting note, James Villiers portrays Bill Tanner, Chief of Staff. The character is seen running the department because in real life Bernard Lee was too ill to participate as M (he died while the film was being shot, in fact). Villiers plays Tanner as an uptight authority

figure who disapproves of Bond's antics, despite Fleming's novels depicting Tanner as Bond's only real friend at MI6. The screen incarnation of the character would reappear during Pierce Brosnan and Daniel Craig's tenures. Coincidentally, Villiers had played the villain in the 007-inspired *Some Girls Do* (1969) which starred Richard Johnson (who was on the shortlist to play James Bond in *Dr. No*).

"Love a Drive in the Country, Don't You?"

To keep costs under control and nervous United Artists executives at ease, the onscreen spectacle in *For Your Eyes Only* is presented in a relatively low-key note.

Debutant Glen proves to be a worthwhile addition to the pantheon of Bond directors. He has a very distinct cinematic eye reminiscent of past 007 filmmakers like Peter Hunt and Terence Young. Many of his compositions are surprisingly subtle in execution.

The opening scene in the cemetery could have been for the start of a new Bond actor's tenure had Moore proven too hard to get. Even the shot of Bond's Walther PPK in the sand, before the camera spotlights the ill-fated Countess Lisl von Schlaf (Cassandra Harris), has a distinct, almost dreamlike look.

In the action stakes, there are at least two excellent chase sequences. After the destruction of his Lotus Esprit Turbo, Bond and Melina outrun Gonzales' men in her yellow Citroen CV2, a rather different kind of 007 vehicle. Racing though the backroads of Spain to the accompaniment of Bill Conti's score, it's a fun set-piece. Later, Bond is chased by some of Locque's men, and there is a thrilling ski segment wherein he does everything from causing skiers to fall to damaging property to skiing at full speed down a bobsleigh run. It's a standout action sequence, and my favorite scene in the movie.

The rest of the film has smaller action segments, including Bond and Melina's trip to the wreck of the *St. Georges* and Columbo's raid on Kristatos' Albanian drug processing plant.

The final raid on Kristatos' hideout is another standout moment, with Bond scaling the sheer Trinity Rock to reach the monastery at the top. Making his way up, the sound of the wind is the only thing we hear on the soundtrack, and we get a real sense that Bond is entirely on his own and precariously exposed. When a guard spots him and begins knocking out his climbing pitons, Bond makes impromptu use of his shoelaces to pulley himself up the rope, knowing that as the bad guy loosens each piton he comes ever closer to falling to his death. Rick Sylvester performed the dangerous drops, while Derek Meddings built a special rig to make sure the fall wouldn't cause a severe jolt to the performer. Glen also uses, for the first time, his recurring technique of having pigeons come out of nowhere at a startling moment (he uses this trick at some point in all his Bond films). In this case, it happens when Bond is scaling the rockface - he reaches into a crack and one flies out, almost making him fall.

Most famous for composing the *Rocky* theme, Conti seems an unlikely choice of Bond composer. Due to issues with the British tax authorities, series regular John Barry was unable to be involved on this occasion. Instead, he recommended Conti as his replacement. Conti's score has a distinct '80s vibe with brass, horns, synthesizers and disco-ish melodies. The standout cues are *A Drive in the Country* and *Runaway*, both of which add energy and excitement to their respective chase sequences. Some of Conti's low-key themes - like Bond's beach stroll with the Countess after their night together and his encounter with Melina at the undersea ruins - are also distinct and memorable. It's very underrated among Bond soundtracks.

The title song, a powerful romantic melody sung by Sheena Easton, is excellent - one of the very best Bond themes. Title designer Maurice Binder and Glen both felt Easton's distinct and striking look deserved to be visible onscreen. As a result, Easton was the first singer to appear in the opening credits, mouthing her lyrics amidst the visuals. Binder's aqua look and underwater theme work superbly alongside the lyrics and Easton's presence.

"By Tomorrow, We'll be Good Friends"

Moving away from the fantasy-laden spectacles of the previous two Bond films, screenwriters Richard Maibaum and Michael G. Wilson (himself a future Bond producer) strive to make this 007 adventure feel like it's taking place in the real world. While Moore's persona is characteristic, the themes around him are a little different.

The ATAC fulfills a similar purpose as the Lektor decoding machine in *From Russia with Love* (1963). Both are top-secret devices which can alter the balance of military power - the Lektor could decode Russian communications between Moscow and Russian embassies, while the ATAC can render an entire country's navy ineffective against its enemies.

Much of the plot takes elements from two Ian Fleming short stories: 'Risico' and 'For Your Eyes Only', both of which appeared in his short story compilation under the latter title and were adapted into daily comic strips by the 'Daily Express' the following year. This keeps the tone directly in Fleming's world, like in the dinner scene where Kristatos and Bond discuss the particulars of the food and drink they're about to consume. Conversations like this could be seen in many of Fleming's Bond books. Another element is borrowed from the novel 'Goldfinger' in the scene where Bond and Q try to piece together Locque's identity by using an identigraph.

There are also several throwbacks to *On Her Majesty's Secret Service*, such as the pre-credits scene which opens with Bond visiting the grave of his wife Tracy. He is picked up by a helicopter which is supposed to take him to HQ, but the pilot is electrocuted and a mysterious bald villain in a motorized wheelchair with a cat takes control of the whirlybird, trying to crash it and Bond into a nearby abandoned gasworks. Bond regains the upper hand, and uses the chopper to scoop up the unnamed villain and dump him down a nearby chimney stack. While not explicitly stated, we're meant to infer the bald bad guy is Blofeld and the scene shows Bond's final revenge against him. It represents a giant middle finger at Kevin McClory, whose constant legal shenanigans regarding his *Thunderball* remake were an annoyance to the EON team. A similar *OHMSS* reference occurs when Bond is walking on the beach with Countess von Schlaf. The two of them are dressed in almost identical clothing as Lazenby and Diana Rigg in the pre-credits sequence of *OHMSS*.

The Cold War backdrop is played out through the characters of Kristatos and Columbo. Both outwardly oppose communism, but Kristatos is revealed as a friend of Moscow and Hoxha's Albania. Under the guise of a capitalist businessman, he's been gaining great influence while protecting his illegal activities and presenting himself as an ally of the West. There is a nice moment of détente when Bond faces General Gogol (Walter Gotell) who arrives in Greece to pick up the ATAC from Kristatos. Bond comes up with a creative way of destroying the device so that neither side can get their hands on it - "that's détente," he declares. "*You* don't have, *I* don't have it!" Gogol walks away laughing philosophically. In the current military climate, it would be nice if the word détente could return to the global lexicon and be spoken frequently!

"This Bond is For Your Eyes Only"
Premiering on June 27th 1981, *For Your Eyes Only* was a box-office success, grossing $194 million worldwide, with $52 million coming from the U.S. Critically, it received good notices and was generally popular.

Easton's title track was also a success, ending up at #4 on the American charts and #8 in Britain. The movie was also adapted as a comic book by Marvel, published as Issue #19 of the 'Marvel Comics Super Special' and re-released in the fall of 1981 as a two-issue series.

For Your Eyes Only marks a soft transition within the series. It was the first of Glen's five consecutive 007 entries which came out at two-year intervals for the rest of the decade. With its subdued plot, interesting characters, good performances and memorable score, it recalibrates the series in an interesting way.

Glen said, in his excellent 2001 autobiography 'For My Eyes Only', that the film was one of his favorites. He said that while working on it he had been initially single-minded but learned to "quickly adapt." Like Bond being forced to adapt when his gadget-laden Lotus is destroyed, it was an ideal time to adapt and refocus the series in general. This refocus carried on through Moore's final two films and reached its crescendo with Timothy Dalton's two instalments at the end of the decade. All the '80s entries, starting with *For Your Eyes Only*, fit into that reality… and if you don't believe me, I'll buy you an ice cream!

THE GOSPEL ACCORDING TO
Spinäl Täp

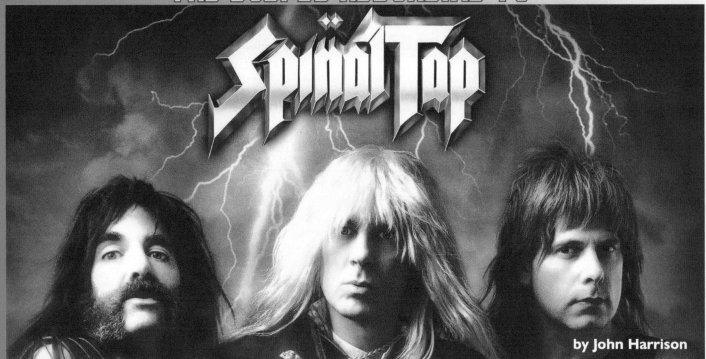

by John Harrison

Few films have been able to blur and blend the lines between fantasy and reality as effectively, and memorably, as Rob Reiner's rock and roll mockumentary *This Is Spinal Tap* (1984). When it was released in the United States, so convinced were many viewers that what they were watching was a genuine documentary, record stores reported kids coming in requesting copies of Spinal Tap's older records, and radio stations received calls requesting the band be given airtime. Of course, in 1984 there was no internet for information to be quickly disseminated and verified, so it was much easier to manipulate the media and keep up an illusion for longer. With a screenplay that was largely improvised by Reiner and the central cast, *This Is Spinal Tap* follows the fictional group, an aging hard rock outfit from England, as they embark on an American tour in support of their new album *Smell the Glove*. Having been around since the '60s, dabbling in everything from Beatles-esque pop to

psychedelia in their quest for stardom, Spinal Tap deal with all the pitfalls of a weary, low-level rock band trying their hardest to stay relevant in a fickle industry. Concerts are cancelled due to lack of ticket sales, no one turns up for their in-store appearances, stage effects go embarrassingly wrong, and their record label refuses to release *Smell the Glove* unless they agree to change the cover, which they deem highly offensive and sexist ("What's wrong with being sexy?" one of the band members asks in response).

Whether it's by default or the result of two decades of rock and roll excess, the members of Spinal Tap are not the most intellectual of men, though they would probably like to think otherwise. Founding duo David St. Hubbins (Michael McKean) and Nigel Tufnel (Christopher Guest) share guitar and vocal duties, with bassist Derek Smalls (Harry Shearer) completing the band's formidable front line. Filling out the line-up is keyboardist Viv Savage (David Kaff) and Mick Shrimpton (R. J. Parnell) as the latest in a revolving door of drummers, most of whom seem to have fallen victim to some bizarre mishap (one dies in a mysterious gardening accident, another spontaneously combusts, while yet another chokes to death on vomit… someone else's vomit).

The origins of *This Is Spinal Tap* date back to 1979, when Rob Reiner and Michael McKean put together a sketch for a television special called *The T.V. Show*. In what was intended as a spoof of live rock music shows like *The Midnight Special* and *Don Kirshner's in Concert*, *The T.V. Show* skit saw Spinal Tap introduced by Reiner in character as the legendary disc jockey Wolfman Jack, and performing a song called *Rock 'n' Roll Nightmare*. At this early stage, the Spinal Tap line-up already consisted of the core trio of McKean, Guest and Shearer. McKean and Guest had been friends since their late '60s college days and had dabbled in music together, so they already had some experience and skills to draw upon. During the filming of *The T.V. Show* segment, some of the actors received minor burns from a stage effect which went wrong, and as they were waiting around during a break in production, McKean and Guest began to improvise dialogue and riff against each other, establishing the basis of their Spinal Tap characters and personalities then and there.

When Rob Reiner was subsequently given $60,000 to develop a screenplay for a Spinal Tap film, it quickly became obvious that, if the idea was to work effectively, it would need to be spontaneous and largely improvised rather than tightly scripted. Instead of a screenplay, Reiner, McKean, Guest and Shearer filmed a short demo reel to shop around, the project eventually getting backed by veteran television producer Norman Lear. Filming took place over a five-week period at various locations across Los Angeles County, including the Six Flags Magic Mountain amusement park in Valencia. For the scene where Spinal Tap visit the grave of Elvis Presley at Graceland in Memphis, Tennessee, a mock-up of Presley's grave site was built and taken to a park in Altadena, California, for filming.

There's a multitude of highlights to *This Is Spinal Tap*, and in fact at only 82 minutes there is very little fat to it (Reiner had over 100 hours of footage in which to choose highlights from). Every fan has their own favourite

moments, whether it's Nigel Tufnel trying to rationalise the uselessness of an amplifier that goes up to 11 instead of 10, Derek Smalls setting off the airport metal detector thanks to his ludicrous genital enhancement, the band getting totally lost on their short walk from the dressing room to the stage, or any number of other memorable scenes and passages of quotable dialogue spoken deadpan straight. Still others love the movie for its music, with songs like *Big Bottom*, *Tonight I'm Gonna Rock You Tonight*, *Sex Farm* and *Heavy Duty*, showing that Spinal Tap could deliver anthemic, sexually-charged hard rock numbers as good as most real metal bands that were packing arenas at that time (their music and style seems to be a mix of Manowar, KISS, Black Sabbath and Saxon).

All of the performers in *This Is Spinal Tap* disappear completely into their characters. It's doubtful many in the audience would have recognised David St. Hubbins as being the same guy who played Lenny on *Laverne &*

Shirley the previous decade, and while Harry Shearer had already worked on *Saturday Night Live* as both a writer and performer, he was not yet the famous figure he became from providing multiple character voices on *The Simpsons*. Casting himself as documentarian Marty Di Bergi, Rob Reiner proves himself just as assured and invaluable in front of the camera as he is behind it, providing the perfect grounding point for all the lunacy taking place around him (*This Is Spinal Tap* was the directorial debut for the actor and television writer). Amongst the supporting cast, Patrick Macnee provides the most familiar face, playing Sir Denis Eton-Hogg, the president of Spinal Tap's label Polymer Records. You can also spot future *The Nanny* star Fran Drescher and David Letterman's long-time band leader Paul Shaffer as members of Polymer's promotional team, and Billy Crystal gets a few brief seconds playing Marty the Mime ("Mime is money").

Assembled by a trio of editors, *This Is Spinal Tap* is expertly

constructed to resemble a legitimate documentary, with cinematographer Peter Smokler often employing handheld cameras to capture a cinéma vérité feel, and there are a couple of very convincing sequences which see the band performing on television as their much younger selves, in both the British Invasion and psychedelia periods of the '60s.

The inspiration for the film's infamous Stonehenge sequence came from legendary British heavy metal pioneers Black Sabbath. By 1983, having lost both original singer Ozzy Osborne and his replacement Ronnie James Dio, Sabbath were at a crossroad in their career. In a move that surprised many, they brought in former Deep Purple front man Ian Gillan, who claims he agreed to join the band during a big night out on the booze! The Gillan/Sabbath experiment only lasted for one album, 1983's *Born Again*, and when the band began planning a tour to support the record, they decided that a replica of Stonehenge would make a suitably eerie stage design. Unfortunately, they built their replica to exact scale, which was fine when they played larger arenas, but for a lot of the shows on the tour, the Stonehenge set was either too big to even fit on the stage or it took up so much space that the band members were left with no more than a couple of feet between the prop and the front edge of the stage! According to Sabbath's lead guitarist Tony Iommi, in his autobiography 'Iron Man', the initial concept for the Stonehenge stage set came from bassist Geezer Butler, who simply told the set designer to make it life-size without realising just how huge the monument was. Butler, in his defence, claims the idea came from their then-manager, Don Arden (father of Ozzy Osborne's wife Sharon), but he does admit that it was him who told someone who was working on *This Is Spinal Tap* all about the Stonehenge set and the problems which came with it. Rob Reiner and crew obviously saw the potential humour in the situation, but took it in the opposite direction, with hilarious results (the decision to make the replica monument so small in the film was also likely a financial one).

This is Spinal Tap was met with excellent reviews, with many critics instantly claiming it one of the funniest films ever made, and it made many of the ten best lists for that year. Commercially, the film was a moderate success at the time, earning roughly double its US $2 million budget during its limited original theatrical release. In many ways, the movie's level of success was perfect for helping it maintain its mystique for a while longer. The illusion of Spinal Tap as a real band was reinforced via some rather clever promotional tactics, which included shooting an MTV-styled music video for the song *Hell Hole* from the film's soundtrack, the latter of which was released by Polydor Records and packaged as a legitimate band album, with an inner lyric sleeve and bogus ads for previous Tap LPs like *Brain-Hammer*, *The Sun Never Sweats,* and the infamous *Shark Sandwich* (which, as Di Bergi reminds the band in the film, was summed up by one reviewer in just two words: "Shit Sandwich"). The core trio of McKean, Guest, and Shearer also frequently conducted television and radio interviews while staying completely within their Spinal Tap characters, and there was a large trade paperback book published, 'Inside Spinal Tap' by Peter Occhiogrosso (Arbor House, 1985), which was formatted less like a traditional "making of" book and more like an illustrated scrapbook and biographical history of the band.

Like a lot of cult films, it was on its subsequent home video release that *This is Spinal Tap* really found its audience, its influence slowly growing until it became a part of pop culture mythology. As the film's following grew, fans sought out bootleg videotapes containing hours of outtakes, and 1992 saw Spinal Tap release a new studio album, *Break Like the Wind*, as well as making an appearance on *The Simpsons* and filming a series of television commercials in Australia for a food snack called Rock 'N' Rolls (similar to Hot Pockets).

While it found popularity amongst most in the industry, *This Is Spinal Tap* wasn't completely embraced by musicians, especially those within the hard rock and metal communities, which the film took specific aim at. In the November 1984 issue of the British pop magazine 'No. 1', KISS bassist and vocalist Gene Simmons was given a VHS of the movie to watch in his motel room while KISS were touring the country. Asked to them provide some

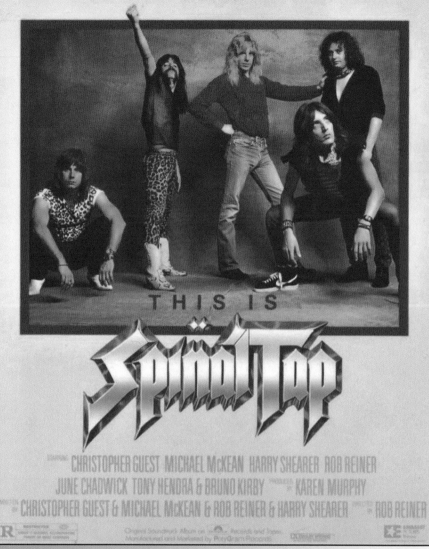

"THE FUNNIEST ROCK MOVIE EVER MADE."
Merrill Shindler—Los Angeles Magazine

"HILARIOUS... SENDS UP WHAT THE BEATLES STARTED WITH 'A HARD DAYS NIGHT.'"
Bruce Williamson—Playboy

"DON'T MISS IT...ONE OF THE FUNNIEST MOVIES"
Stephen Shaefer—US Magazine

THIS IS

Spïnäl Tap

STARRING CHRISTOPHER GUEST · MICHAEL McKEAN · HARRY SHEARER · ROB REINER JUNE CHADWICK · TONY HENDRA & BRUNO KIRBY PRODUCED BY KAREN MURPHY WRITTEN BY CHRISTOPHER GUEST & MICHAEL McKEAN & ROB REINER & HARRY SHEARER DIRECTED BY ROB REINER

feedback on the film, Simmons was less than enthusiastic, some of the incidents and caricatures in the movie clearly hitting a bit close to home:

"I consider there are some things that shouldn't be made fun of - unless they're made fun of by the same people. I can make fun of myself, but you try and make fun of me and I'll kick your ass. It's well done but I *hate* the fact that they're making a comedy out of something I consider serious."

Of course, Gene's disdain for *This Is Spinal Tap* didn't stop him from later stealing an infamous line from *Big Bottom* - "The bigger the cushion, the sweeter the pushin'" - for his own song *Spit*, which wound up on KISS' 1992 album *Revenge*.

FURTHER RECOMMENDED VIEWING:

THE COMIC STRIP PRESENTS: BAD NEWS TOUR
(1983/Directed by Sandy Johnson)

"I could play *Stairway to Heaven* when I was twelve. Jimmy Page didn't actually write it until he was twenty-two. I think that says quite a lot."

Pre-dating *This Is Spinal Tap* by a full year, this hilarious episode of the UK comedy series *The Comic Strip Presents* features many of the cast of *The Young Ones* playing members of Bad News, a wannabe working class British metal band dealing with the realities of putting up with each other and life on the road as they embark on a tour in their cramped, decrepit old van. Like Spinal Tap, Bad News would later cross over into real life with some performances and personal appearances by the actors in character. Unlike Spinal Tap, most people recognized it as a send-up from the start.

HEAVY METAL PARKING LOT
(1986/Directed by John Heyn and Jeff Krulik)

This short documentary follows a group of young hard rock fans who assemble and party in the parking lot of the Capital Centre in Landover, Maryland, on May 31, 1986, as they prepare for a Judas Priest concert taking place that evening (with Dokken the supporting act). *Heavy Metal Parking Lot* quickly became a cult film and an in-demand bootleg VHS, providing an honest look at a popular ritual performed by teens outside concert venues around the world, in an era when they couldn't rely on social media to keep themselves entertained or occupied.

THE DECLINE OF WESTERN CIVILIZATION PART II: THE METAL YEARS
(1988/Directed by Penelope Spheeris)

Any doubts that *This Is Spinal Tap* went a bit too far with unrealistic characterization should get wiped away with a viewing of this documentary from the future director of *Wayne's World* (1992). Looking at the heavy metal scene of the '80s, with particular focus on the hair/glam metal movement that was then dominating the Sunset Strip in Los Angeles, *The Decline of Western Civilization Part II: The Metal Years* gives us such sights as an intoxicated Chris Holmes from W.A.S.P. gulping vodka while floating in his swimming pool, Paul Stanley from KISS being interviewed on a bed surrounded by half-naked girls, a forgotten band called Odin cavorting with groupies in a hot tub while predicting they will soon be millionaires and more popular than Led Zeppelin or The Doors, and a member of a band with the awesome name of Wet Cherry, who is 100% convinced he is destined to make it big (if he ever did, it sure wasn't in the music industry!)

THE SIMPSONS: "THE OTTO SHOW"
(1992/Directed by Wes Archer)

Spinal Tap make a significant guest appearance in this classic, third-season episode of *The Simpsons*. Bart dreams of becoming a rock star after he and Millhouse attend a typically disastrous Spinal Tap concert in Springfield. Helping Bart to learn guitar is burned-out bus driver Otto, who comes to live with the Simpsons after losing his job.

ANVIL! THE STORY OF ANVIL
(2008/Directed by Sacha Gervasi)

The closest you are likely to come to a real-life *This Is Spinal Tap* would be this documentary on Canadian heavy metal band Anvil, who in the early '80s were poised to lead the great thrash metal charge along with the likes of Metallica, Slayer, Megadeath and Anthrax but sadly became left in the dust and largely forgotten about, apart from a small band of devoted cult followers. In turns hilarious, inspirational, and sad, *Anvil! The Story of Anvil* looks at co-founders Steve 'Lips' Kudlow (guitar/vocals) and Robb Reiner (drums) as they attempt to mount a European tour in 2005 (for which they have to take leave from their mundane day jobs). The chaos of the tour culminates with Anvil headlining the big 'Monsters of Transylvania' rock concert, which attracts a crowd of only 174 to a venue that holds 10,000. Anvil drummer Robb Reiner is no relation to the director of *This Is Spinal Tap*, though it's hard not to contemplate the irony of the coincidence.

HONKYTONK MAN

by David Flack

When fans discuss their favourite Clint Eastwood films, one that is virtually guaranteed not to be mentioned is the Depression-set *Honkytonk Man* (1982). It is not well liked by most of the star's fans. I do not share that opinion; in fact, I rate it quite highly. For me it's a Top 10 Eastwood film.

The plot is quite simple. It follows the story of Whit (Kyle Eastwood), a teenager whose family are struggling to make ends meet in '30s America. One day, a car crashes through their farm and it turns out the driver is a somewhat inebriated Red Stovall (Clint Eastwood), the brother of Whit's mother. Uncle Red is a budding country-and-western singer who is passing through on his way to Nashville, hoping to get his big breakthrough in the music industry. He has managed to get a spot performing at the Grand Ole Opry, a weekly singing event held in the city. Red is pretty booze-sodden, so decides to spend a few days with the family before heading on.

While there, he forms a bond with his nephew and realises the youngster will be a useful companion for the long journey, especially as he can drive. Red asks if Whit is allowed to accompany him. His mother reluctantly agrees because she knows her brother is reckless. She also knows Red is ill with tuberculosis and could do with someone to take care of him. During the journey to Nashville with his somewhat unorthodox uncle, Whit learns some of the facts of life.

Honkytonk Man is basically a road movie and an entertaining one at that. It is episodic in nature, with segments along the way which alternate between warm, funny and poignant. An early scene, showing the family dining and conversing at the kitchen table, sets the characters up nicely. It's pretty smooth running from there on in.

Whit's parents, Emmy and Virgil (Verna Bloom and Matt Clark), seem like decent people who are trying to bring their children up as best they can in difficult times. The grandpa (John McIntire) is probably a little senile and likes to reminisce about past, more enjoyable times. Whit is getting restless at home and has a yearning for adventure. Red notices this, and believes he and the boy can be useful to each other on the journey. He is uneasy with family life and is definitely a loner and a drifter.

On the road, they have various scrapes and misadventures as they head towards Nashville.

One has to wonder why *Honkytonk Man* isn't liked very much by fans of the star. I think the answer to that is that audiences weren't ready to see someone like Eastwood - who had established himself as a tough and heroic type - playing a deeply flawed, seriously ill and vulnerable character like Red Stovall. We learn early in the proceedings that he is ill and susceptible to changeable mood swings. We soon realise this isn't going to be a rags-to-riches story. Yes, he makes it to Nashville and gets a shot at fame and fortune, but it doesn't exactly run smoothly to plan. '80s films tended to be more upbeat and positive, not fashionably bleak like a lot of '70s movies, so audiences (especially Eastwood fans) must have found *Honkytonk*

Man something of a culture shock. It probably seemed strange to them to watch a film in which Eastwood's character doesn't kill anybody.

Now, I like Eastwood films in general, and I particularly like this one. It marks a risky but commendable change of pace for the star. It made me sit up and realise he can really act; he demonstrates a side we haven't really seen before. Clint might have been tempted to cast an established country singer in the main role (Johnny Cash or Kris Kristofferson, for example) and just settled for directing, but he didn't and I for one am glad. Although they play uncle and nephew here, the chemistry between Eastwood and his real-life son Kyle is solid, and helps the film immensely. Their natural relationship helps, and I'm not sure Kyle would have come off so well opposite a different star.

The million-dollar question for people watching for the first time is: is Eastwood as strong at singing as acting? The honest answer is no, though he makes up for his limited vocal ability in other ways. Clint's most famous character 'Dirty' Harry Callahan once uttered: "Man's got to know his limitations", and the actor seems to keep that mantra in mind here. That said, he had dabbled in singing during his *Rawhide* days, recording an album of cowboy songs, and he'd appeared (and sang) in the musical *Paint Your Wagon* (1969). He didn't exactly embarrass himself in the latter, but looked distinctly uneasy and was outshone by Lee Marvin. He looks more assured and at ease in *Honkytonk Man* but is still not quite strong enough to carry all the notes. I should make it clear he doesn't embarrass himself; he's just not as good in the singing stakes as a real country musician would have been. He gets by thanks to his professionalism and canniness - if you pay attention, you'll realise there really isn't much singing by Eastwood, just snippets here and there. The film mostly fades out from his singing scenes rather than dwelling on the whole song.

When Red reaches Nashville and performs at the trials, he is stopped by coughing fits which result in him being rejected to play at the concert. A sympathetic record producer gets him to record his songs in a studio, and says "We'll see if we can find a song that will get you noticed." Again, we only see and hear little snippets, never the whole song. The song which shares its title with the film is the only one we get to hear in full, in a scene where the acting is as important as the song itself. It's perhaps the most poignant moment in the movie. While performing, Red has a bad coughing fit and the backing musician Smoky (played by real life country singer Marty Robbins) has to take over to finish the song. We see Red struggling off the recording set, fighting a coughing fit helplessly and hopelessly. Meanwhile, he hears Smoky performing his song, and realises it's being sung well and that he will be remembered for it. It's a superb, moving moment of bittersweet realisation, one of the best pieces

of acting I've ever seen from Eastwood. Little Kyle Eastwood adds to it with his very convincing look of concern (a bit of Method acting going on here, maybe, watching his real-life father acting gravely ill?) There's an added poignancy when ones reflects that Marty Robbins died of a heart attack after cardiac surgery weeks before *Honkytonk Man* was released. Robbins sings the song perfectly, and his version of it reached number 10 in the US country music charts (it was his last hit). On the other occasions where Eastwood has sung on film (e.g. *Kelly's Heroes*, *Every Which Way But Loose* and *Bronco Billy*), he duetted with a proper established singer to helps cover his inadequacies.

Honkytonk Man's climatic scenes are up there with *Million Dollar Baby* (2004) and *Gran Torino* (2008) for poignant endings to Eastwood films. As for the supporting players, Eastwood casts actors he had used many times such as Matt Clark and Verna Bloom, but most of the minor characters have little more than fleeting roles. The two Eastwoods remain the main focus throughout. Kyle is good as young Whit (the character is meant to be a little under 16, and Kyle was 14 in real life), and I have to say it's a shame he never played any other significant roles. Prior to this, he'd had two uncredited bit-parts (in *The Outlaw Josey Wales* [1976] and *Bronco Billy* [1980]), but most of his career has been spent in the music industry. He even scored a handful of soundtracks for his father, including *Letters from Iwo Jima* (2006), *Gran Torino* (2008) and *Invictus* (2009).

Of the rest of the cast, John McIntire plays the grandpa who accompanies them for some of the trip. The role was originally offered to (and turned down by) James Stewart, which would have been interesting. Among the other supporting players are Barry Corbin as an untrustworthy businessman who owes Stovall money, Jerry Hardin as a county town sheriff, Joe Regalbuto as a sympathetic record studio producer, and, best of all, Tim Thomerson in a brief but amusing cameo as a motorcycle cop. Special mention for Alexa Kenin as Marlene, a young girl who is offered as 'payment' in place of the money owed and who dreams of stardom in Nashville. Red declines but she stows away with them and ends up joining them on their journey until she is ditched by Red (she later finds and joins up with them again). Sadly, three years after appearing in this film she was found dead in her Manhattan apartment, aged just 23 - cause unknown.

Country musicians making cameo appearances include Ray Price, Shelly West, Porter Wagoner, and Merle Travis. Despite being considered a lesser Eastwood film, *Honkytonk Man* is an enjoyable, easily watchable film, a real change from most of Clint's action output. With it not going down well with critics and audiences, Clint leapt right back into familiar territory next by reviving Harry Callahan for *Sudden Impact* (1983). He didn't delve into non-action cinema again until *Bird* (1988, director-only) and *White Hunter, Black Heart* (1990). It's a shame, as *Honkytonk Man* is a commendable foray into something different, a chance to show off his dramatic talents as well as doing his own guitar and piano-playing and (admittedly moderate) singing.

Made for an estimated $2 million, the film grossed worldwide just over double that, so it wasn't among his biggest earners. It contains some of Eastwood's best acting, and is preferable to some of his other uncharacteristic, gentler offerings like the rather dull *Bronco Billy* and *Space Cowboys* (2000). More recent reviews of the film suggest a re-evaluation and re-appreciation is underway, which is encouraging as it is an unfairly underrated piece of entertainment.

(I dedicate this article to my late father, John Flack [7th May 1936 - 14th October 2022], a Clint Eastwood and country music fan. We all love and miss you dad, always will. Thanks for being a good husband, father, brother and grandad. See you later).

"...not far short of magnificent"
—NEW MUSICAL EXPRESS

"Not often does a film smack so roundly of family entertainment"
—SUNDAY TIMES

The boy is on his way to becoming a man. The man is on his way to becoming a legend.

Clint Eastwood and Kyle Eastwood

Honkytonk Man

Clint Eastwood and Kyle Eastwood in "Honkytonk Man" Executive Producer Fritz Manes · Screenplay by Clancy Carlile. based upon his novel Produced and Directed by Clint Eastwood

FANNY & ALEXANDER

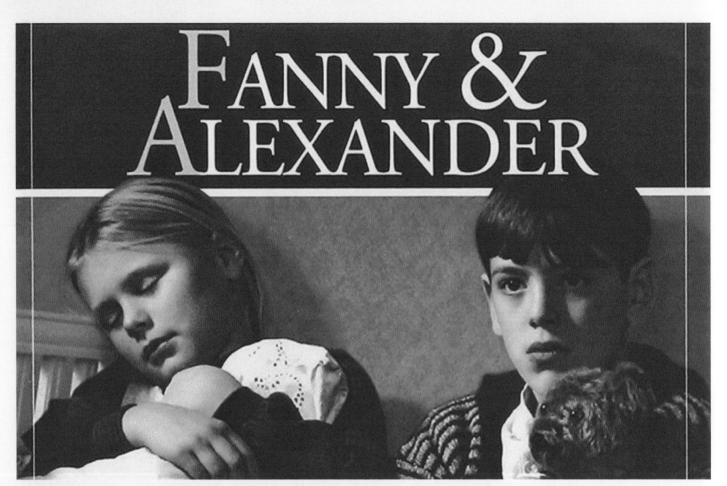

Dr. Andrew C. Webber immerses himself in a master filmmaker's dream world.

At the risk of sounding like a *Top of the Pops* presenter, let me start by observing that in the recently published BFI critics' poll of the Top 100 films of all time, Ingmar Bergman's much-admired *Persona* appears at number 18 and is his only entry in the chart.

A list compiled by contemporary directors is traditionally run alongside the critics' poll. Interestingly, the directors' poll places *Persona* at number 9. *The Seventh Seal* also makes an appearance (at number 72) and *Fanny and Alexander* - Bergman's epic from 1982 - slips in at number 53. Taking the directors' poll as a benchmark, *Fanny and Alexander* is one of the ten greatest films of the '80s (there are twelve '80s entries on the list, with Abbas Kiarostami's *Close-Up* occupying the highest position at number 11). I think what we should take from this is that *Fanny and Alexander* is very much a "filmmakers' film", which raises two obvious questions: as '80s aficionados, should we regard Bergman's film (which he also wrote) as one of the decade's bona fide masterpieces? And more importantly, is it worth over three hours of our time?

Fanny and Alexander is a lovingly crafted, semi-autobiographical account of Bergman's early years growing up in a highly theatrical, wealthy upper-class family in Uppsala in 1907. It was originally made for Swedish TV and had a running time over five hours. It marked the director's return to Sweden after years of exile following unfounded tax dodging allegations. In the movie, the matriarchal grandmother Helena Ekdahl (Gunn Wållgren) holds everything together and dominates the early part (*"Don't scowl,"* she orders one of her servants). This opening section is set over the Christmas period, replete with all sorts of scenes which have made the film a festive favourite - huge banquets, gift-giving, a trip to see the Christmas play, some cavorting in the snow, and typically Swedish customs like conga-ing throughout the house and pillow fights.

Helena is a widow with three sons - academic Carl (Börje Ahlstedt) whose character remains relatively undeveloped; ailing theatre actor and manager Oscar (Allan Edwall) and charismatic restaurant proprietor Gustav (Jarl Kulle) - all of whom are married with varying degrees of success. Perhaps unbeknown to them is the fact that Helena is conducting a late-flowering affair with a charismatic Jewish antiquarian named Isak (Erland Josephson, a Bergman regular). The scene early on where she looks round carefully before embracing him to thank him for the Christmas gift she has received is a finely judged moment.

Little does she know that one of her sons will die during the season, triggering the movie's shift into much darker territory. Helena's daughter-in-law Emilie (Ewa Fröling) then falls in love with the local puritanical bishop Vergerus (Jan Malmsjö) and, after an "o'er hasty" marriage, takes her children (the eponymous Fanny and Alexander) to live with him in a world far removed from the luxuries and gaiety of grandma's house. The role of Emilie was originally intended for Bergman's one-time lover Liv Ullmann, who turned it down for scheduling reasons, leaving the similar-looking Fröling to assume the role.

At this point, the movie - which starts off very much like something by Dickens (with added touches of Shakespeare) - begins to feel more like a Thomas Hardy novel with hypocritical religious characters, suggestions of the supernatural (the story features several ghosts), females in peril and threatening rivers ever present. It becomes increasingly melodramatic and gothic (there are even bars on the children's bedroom window). It's interesting - worrying, even - to note that much of this is allegedly based on Bergman's childhood!

Alexander (Bertil Guve), the film's Bergman-as-a-child figure, comes into direct conflict with his new stepfather, culminating in a brutal caning sequence which is all the more gruelling since the bishop's sister Henrietta (Kerstin Tidelius) holds down Alexander's neck while her brother lays into him.

The children are saved in almost fairy-tale style by good old Isak, who ferrets them back to safety, but not before Alexander has a strange encounter with the voice of a puppet God - actually the androgynous and reclusive Ismael (Stina Ekblad) - which is homoerotically charged and decidedly ambiguous.

As well as everything else which takes place in the film (and this is a movie in which *a great deal* happens) sex certainly features high among Bergman's concerns, especially in the representation of Gustav who has a very open relationship with his wife. She even appears to encourage him to conduct an affair with buxom servant Maj (Pernilla Wallgren), even though their sex life is represented as being far from frigid. Maj appears to have a soft spot for young Alexander too and, as already noted, grandma is involved with Isak on the side. If all this makes *Fanny and Alexander* sound like an upmarket soap opera, well… I guess that's about right! After all, most soaps deal with families, birth, marriage and death - and this is no exception. In fact, the scene where we hear Emilie's

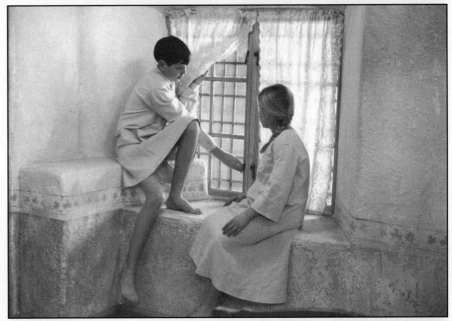

primal screaming following her husband's heart-attack (whilst playing Hamlet, no less) contains the most harrowing sounds this viewer has yet heard on screen. The grotesquery of his final moments, as viewed through the eyes of young Alexander, is haunting and terrifying too.

This is a movie full of love and pain and the whole damned thing, and it's a rich and heady mix, stunningly realised by cinematographer Sven Nykvist who composes scenes with absolute mastery throughout. As shown in his his previous Oscar-winning collaboration with Bergman, *Cries and Whispers* (1972), Nykvist had a Technicolor love of the colour red, and much of *Fanny and Alexander* is sumptuously bathed in varying hues of the colour. These contrast brilliantly with the austere whites and greys of the bishop's house, where we move for the latter part of the film (and even that literally explodes into red in the fiery climax, as does the final frame of the movie).

If all this sounds a little po-faced, we should not forget that *Fanny and Alexander* also includes scenes where a key character sets light to his farts, a bed breaks farcically whilst a couple are over-excitedly making love on it, and a statue comically appears to come to life and dance.

The film was extremely well received at the 1984 Oscars, deservedly winning 4 awards - Best Foreign Film, Best Cinematography, Best Costumes (Marik Vos) and Best Art Direction (Anna Asp). Had it been entered for Best Film it would arguably have won that - rivals being the eventual winner *Terms of Endearment, The Big Chill, The Dresser, The Right Stuff*

and *Tender Mercies,* none of which (apart from *The Right Stuff*) have weathered particularly well. The Best Director award that year went to James L. Brooks for *Terms of Endearment* and Horton Foote won the writing award for *Tender Mercies* - neither strikes me as being superior to Bergman's direction or script.

The whole thing is eminently theatrical (it's not just *Hamlet* - *The Tempest,* Strindberg, Ibsen and even Agatha Christie are all there too) and, at the same time, wonderfully cinematic. Alexander's awe of a magic lantern he fires up when the children have been put to bed is an obvious precursor to Bergman's love of cinema and is most definitely based on real life. The acting is a treat, ranging from the extremely stagey, larger-than-life comic turns by Josephson and Kulle to the dark, menacing work done by Jan Malmsjö (his final ghostly appearance comes as a rather shocking surprise). The only real disappointment is that we only really see things from young Alexander's point of view - in spite of her name appearing in the title, his sister Fanny (Pernilla Allwin) hardly gets a look-in and remains a marginal player.

What makes it special, however (and make no mistake, this *is* a very special film) is that it's so full of heart, soul, warmth and humanity. Whilst Bergman's perennial themes of faith and guilt are present and correct, *Fanny and Alexander* is very much in love with life and all its pleasures: fine food, drinking, love, friendship, sex, family, ritual, forgiveness.

One is reminded of the end of *Macbeth* where, having made decisions which have altered his perspective to something utterly nihilistic, Macbeth tragically concludes:

I have lived long enough. My way of life
Is fallen into the sere, the yellow leaf,
And that which should accompany old age,
As honour, love, obedience, troops of friends,
I must not look to have.

In *Fanny and Alexander,* Bergman shows us that the things that matter in life are not, as Cimino suggested on the poster for *Heaven's Gate,* the things which fade. What really matter are the things which unite us, the things which bring us together, the things which can be shared.

This is a hugely life-affirming film, made by an old man (Bergman was 64 at the time and planned to retire afterwards) who seems to be offering a summation of his career - his love of cinema, theatre, art and literature. At the same time, the movie ponders the big themes: mortality, childhood, the consequences of our actions on others, love and faith.

It's a grand statement - an immersive, colourful, rich and enjoyable experience.

A bit, we hope, like life, then.

Three hours well spent - but only on the biggest screen possible.

Michelle Pfeiffer in the '80s

by Michael Campochiaro

At the dawn of the '80s, a 22-year-old actress with only a handful of television credits made her film debut, and hardly anyone noticed. That actress was Michelle Pfeiffer, and within just a few years she would be firmly established on the path to stardom, a path upon which she's been traveling ever since. In a career spanning five decades, Pfeiffer has been one of the biggest, most recognizable names in cinema over that period, starring in more than fifty movies, including signature roles in *The Fabulous Baker Boys* (1989), *Batman Returns* (1992), *The Age of Innocence* (1993), *What Lies Beneath* (2000), *White Oleander* (2002) and *Mother!* (2017). Yet, every superstar begins as an unknown, and it was no different for Pfeiffer when she first graced movie screens in 1980.

Her first two films came out that year, and neither were particularly well-regarded at the time, if they were regarded at all. Supporting roles in the *American Graffiti*-style teen comedy *The Hollywood Knights* and the romantic comedy *Falling in Love Again* didn't exactly point toward the sort of critically acclaimed career she was destined for, but still there are brief glimmers of the star she would soon blossom into, just a few years later in *Grease 2* (1982) and *Scarface* (1983). Interestingly, Pfeiffer's early career trajectory from playing beautiful blonde bombshell roles to the multilayered, complex characters she would become famous for is neatly encapsulated within the

entirety of the '80s. From her first, mostly forgettable films of 1980 to her final film of the decade *The Fabulous Baker Boys* (1989), her ascent to the top tier of actors in Hollywood was complete by decade's end.

From an unknown making her film debut in 1980, to back-to-back Oscar nominations by 1989, the '80s are when Pfeiffer became both a critically lauded actress and a movie star. The impressive roll she was on at decade's end would continue well into the '90s. Beyond that, she has built a lasting career as a respected actor whose thoughtful, organic performances are cherished by generations of fans and critics to this day. Let's start at the beginning and work our way through her '80s filmography.

Early '80s: "I'm free every day, it's in the Constitution"

The television series *Delta House* premiered in 1979. An *Animal House* spinoff about the various shenanigans at the fictitious Faber College's Delta House fraternity, the show didn't last long and was cancelled after twelve episodes. Appearing in all but the pilot episode was a young, sun-kissed, blonde California girl named Michelle Pfeiffer. She played a recurring character whose real name was never identified. Instead, she was only referred to as "The Bombshell." As an absurdly attractive anthropology student, Pfeiffer was mostly called upon to look beautiful in tight sweaters and laugh along at dumb jokes. This bombshell role would set the course for her early work, as she appeared in similar roles during guest spots on *CHiPs* and *Fantasy Island*, as well as another failed series *B.A.D. Cats* in which she played the fantastically named supporting character Samantha 'Sunshine' Jensen whose main duties were, you guessed it, looking gorgeous and laughing at dumb jokes.

Her first several film roles followed suit. In her cinematic debut *The Hollywood Knights* (1980), she was part of a young, up-and-coming ensemble featuring Tony Danza, Robert Wuhl and Fran Drescher. Pfeiffer played another young, sun-kissed, blonde

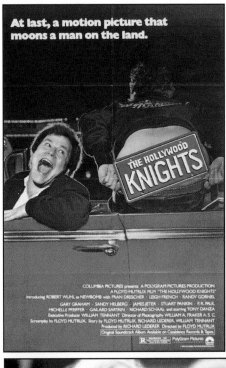

California girl named Suzie Q, an aspiring actress and the girlfriend of Danza's character. It's 1965 and she works as a carhop at Tubby's Drive-In, while dreaming of acting stardom and looking downright dreamy. It's a small, mostly unsubstantial role, but Pfeiffer infuses Suzie with a well-earned vulnerability. She makes the character's ennui palpable with just her eyes, facial expressions and line deliveries, even if the dialogue she's reciting isn't doing nearly as much to convey that as her performance.

After another small role in her next film, the lackluster romantic melodrama *Falling in Love Again* (1980), Pfeiffer made a trio of television movies in 1981 and costarred in the all-star comedy *Charlie Chan and the Curse of the Dragon Queen* (1981). Peter Ustinov was yet another in a long, troubling line of Western actors to play the legendary Chinese detective Chan. Alongside Ustinov, other Hollywood legends like Lee Grant, Angie Dickinson, Roddy McDowell and Brian Keith seem to have had a blast filming this silly comedy-mystery movie. In her supporting role as Cordelia, the adoring fiancée of Chan's grandson Lee Chan (Richard Hatch), Pfeiffer also seems to be having fun. In a film full of over-the-top performances, Grant steals the show every time she's onscreen, but the young, relatively inexperienced Pfeiffer shows early signs of her

impressively deft comedic skills. Cordelia's puppy dog eyes never stray far from the love of her life, fiancé Lee, and the role doesn't offer much in the way of character development, but it's impossible not to be charmed by Pfeiffer's plucky, fun-loving performance. Does it point to her three future Academy Award nominations? Of course not, but it most definitely establishes that Pfeiffer can command the screen with more than just her looks, although she looks adorable and stunning all at once in the film. She would further fine-tune her growing screen presence and star power in her next feature film, in the best role yet of her young career.

Hitting theaters four years after the wildly successful pop culture phenomenon *Grease* (1978), *Grease 2* was destined to fail. Audiences and

GREASE 2

The music and feeling go on forever.

PARAMOUNT PICTURES PRESENTS A ROBERT STIGWOOD/ALLAN CARR PRODUCTION · GREASE 2
Starring MAXWELL CAULFIELD · MICHELLE PFEIFFER · ADRIAN ZMED · LORNA LUFT and DIDI CONN as Frenchy
Special Guest Appearances by EVE ARDEN · SID CAESAR · DODY GOODMAN · TAB HUNTER · CONNIE STEVENS
Choreography by PATRICIA BIRCH · Executive Producer BILL OAKES · Written by KEN FINKLEMAN
Produced by ROBERT STIGWOOD and ALLAN CARR · Directed by PATRICIA BIRCH
READ THE PAPERBACK FROM WANDERER BOOKS · PANAVISION · ORIGINAL SOUNDTRACK ALBUM AVAILABLE ON RSO RECORDS
A PARAMOUNT PICTURE

critics wanted more Danny (John Travolta) and Sandy (Olive Newton-John). Beyond a few returning bit players, what they got instead was a new cast of characters, played by actors yet to establish their names, including Maxwell Caufield, Adrian Zmed, Christopher McDonald and Michelle Pfeiffer. As one of these relative newbies, Pfeiffer scored her first leading role. As Rydell High's leader of the Pink Ladies for 1961, Pfeiffer played Stephanie Zinone, a character who would eventually grow into a cult favorite among fans worldwide, thanks largely to her charismatic performance. From the first moment she appears, during the *Back to School* opening musical number, Pfeiffer is as cool as the other side of the pillow. Stephanie is like Arthur Fonzarelli and Susie Quatro all rolled into one scintillating package. Not only is she afforded the best lines in the movie, but Pfeiffer's memorable delivery transforms these words into iconic moments.

Speaking of iconic, her song and dance routine to *Cool Rider* will always be the film's signature moment, the one you can namedrop to almost anyone with even the slightest pop cultural knowledge and they'll know exactly what you're talking about. Watching Pfeiffer seductively climb and straddle that ladder as she sings of wanting to find a man who will "burn me through and through" is a significant movie moment for fans who grew up watching the film in reruns repeatedly throughout the '80s and '90s. How could it not be? Pfeiffer positively commands the screen. It's also a precursor to another, even bigger musical moment that was still to come in the 1989 film that earned a Best Actress Academy Award nomination, *The Fabulous Baker Boys*. Eventually, a devoted fanbase developed around *Grease 2* turning it into a beloved classic, but initial reviews were mostly negative and the box office receipts disappointing. While Pfeiffer's performance is a clear indication that she had the star power to carry a movie, her career breakout moment would fully arrive with her next film.

Mid '80s: "Don't call me baby"
Brian De Palma's notorious *Scarface* (1983) was a massive production. Directed by De Palma from a script by Oliver Stone, starring Al Pacino and produced by Martin Bregman, *Scarface* was the most prestigious production Pfeiffer had worked on yet. She almost didn't get the role that launched her career. De Palma and Pacino weren't sold on the *Grease 2* star, but Bregman fought for Pfeiffer in the role of Elvira Hancock, the long-suffering wife of Pacino's Cuban gangster Tony Montana. In the end, Bregman was right to have seen what he saw in her for Elvira, as it turned out to be one of the defining roles of her career, and the one that elevated her career to the next level.

In his book 'Opening Wednesday at a Theater or Drive-In Near You', Charles Taylor sums up the impact of

Scarface on Pfeiffer's career: "Michelle Pfeiffer was a star from the moment she descended in that glass elevator in Scarface - although the automatic prejudice that assumes beautiful people can't act means it took a while for people to see she was also an actress." She enters the elevator "Michelle Pfeiffer, 25-year-old actress with a handful of movie roles," and exits as "Michelle Pfeiffer, Movie Star." Taylor captures something essential about how this scene, and this film, impacted her career during the '80s: she was often unfairly categorized as just a "screen beauty." She was also an extremely talented actress, whose acting skills only improved as the decade progressed.

After her breakthrough in Scarface, she didn't appear in cinemas during 1984, but returned with two films that have become cherished cult classics of the '80s, Into the Night and Ladyhawke. In John Landis' Into the Night, Pfeiffer delivers a charismatic performance as the red leather jacket wearing jewel thief Diana, who teams with insomniac aerospace engineer Ed Okin (a delightfully droll Jeff Goldblum) during a wild adventure that takes them all over nighttime Los Angeles. An unlikely pair, both Diana and Ed feel damaged in their own ways, and together they forge a heartfelt connection. Pfeiffer and Goldblum share tremendous chemistry onscreen, and it's a pure delight to journey into the night with them on their madcap adventure. Today, Into the Night is beloved by

zonked wife in *Scarface*, is so beautiful that one is apt not to notice that she has the potential for being a fine comedienne." Canby's half-correct: Pfeiffer displayed the potential for being a fine "comedienne" in the film, but to say these talents are overwhelmed by her looks sounds patently absurd from today's vantage point, and frankly should have sounded absurd from 1985's vantage point, too.

Ladyhawke has taken a similar cult trajectory since 1985. Richard Donner's medieval fantasy film about

star-crossed lovers cursed by a spiteful, evil bishop was another box office failure that eventually found its fanbase on home video in the '80s and '90s. Pfeiffer is perfectly cast as the ethereally beautiful Isabeau, cursed to be a hawk by day while her lover Navarre - a rare heroic role for Rutger Hauer - is transformed against his will into a wolf every night. Andrew Powell's orchestral-meets-progressive-rock score and Matthew Broderick's comic relief are both memorable, but the heart of the story belongs to Pfeiffer's and Hauer's characters. Certainly, the role plays into Pfeiffer's beauty. Yet in this fantasy world, her beauty translates onscreen to warmth and love. With her hair shorn and those oceanic blue eyes gleaming, she projects a calming presence whenever she appears throughout.

Her next two films did little to advance the notion that she was a

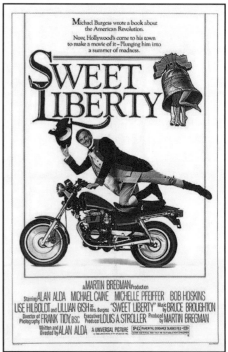

many fans and critics who came to the film via home video over the ensuing decades. At the time of release, it was mostly a nonentity at the box office and received mediocre critical responses. In a review for the 'New York Times', Vincent Canby wasn't much of a fan, but that didn't stop him from giving Pfeiffer a backhanded compliment, writing: "Miss Pfeiffer, last seen as Al Pacino's cocaine-

rising star, but each still offers small pleasures. The first was the midlife crisis comedy *Sweet Liberty* (1986) from writer-director-star Alan Alda. The second, *Amazon Women on the Moon* (1987), was an all-star comedy anthology film that allowed her to utilize the facility for comedy that she'd previously shown in *Grease 2* and *Into the Night*. In *Sweet Liberty*, Pfeiffer plays Faith, an actress in a Hollywood adaptation of Alda's character's historical novel, which is being shot on location where Michael lives and teaches in North Carolina. Struggling in his relationships with a longtime girlfriend and dealing with the stress of caring for an aging mother, Alda's college professor/writer Michael channels his frustrations into excitement for the movie, only to become completely disillusioned with the cynical Hollywood process. Pfeiffer's role is small in terms of screen time but the appropriately named Faith provides Michael with the inspiration he needs to snap himself out of his small college town slumber. It's another role as a beautiful character seen through the eyes a male protagonist, but in *Sweet Liberty* she is afforded a powerful scene that lays bare Faith's own cynicism. She delivers a powerful performance in that moment, and in so doing tugs back a little agency for Faith, at least as much as was possible in a small role in an '80s film.

Late '80s: "You do what you do, right?"

After making waves with *Scarface* in 1983, Pfeiffer had been in some good films that didn't get much buzz, but with *The Witches of Eastwick* (1987) - a cinematic adaptation of John Updike's bestseller - she was once again thrust into the spotlight. This time though, it was as one-third of a female-led cast that includes Cher and Susan Sarandon. Their characters are old friends living normal lives in a sleepy, conservative New England town. Their mundane existence is disrupted by the arrival of a mysterious, mischievous and malevolent stranger who just might be the Devil in disguise, gleefully played by Jack Nicholson. Seven years later, Pfeiffer and Nicholson would costar in another supernatural story, Mike Nichols' excellent *Wolf* (1994), at which point Pfeiffer was already a three-time Oscar nominee and one of the biggest names in the

business. In *The Witches of Eastwick* though, she was still a bit of an upstart, going head-to-head with the legendary Oscar winner Nicholson - and she more than holds her own at every turn. Watching them together in *The Witches of Eastwick* is nothing short of delightful. The entire cast play magnificently off each other. Against Nicholson's devilish antagonist, the women unleash their previously unrealized powers as honest-to-God witches, allowing Pfeiffer, Cher and Sarandon to take their characters on meaningful emotional arcs during the film.

Pfeiffer's portrayal of Sukie, the sweetest and most

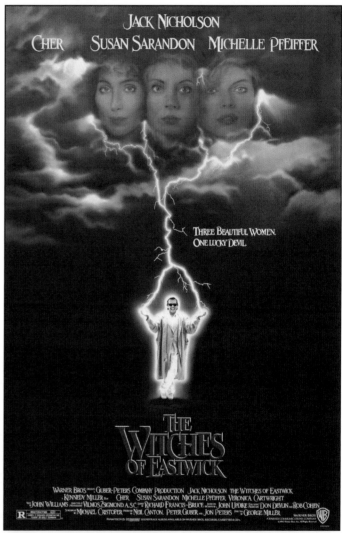

quietly perceptive of the witches, does not always immediately spring to mind when discussing her best performances, but it's a lovely, nuanced bit of acting. She's shy and reserved when we meet her, then brave and determined as she and her friends blossom into impressive sorceresses. Together, they are more than a match for Nicholson's dastardly rogue Daryl Van Horne. Her work alongside other cast luminaries proved without a doubt that she was ready for the big time. Whether or not critics realized this at the time is irrelevant; by the following year she'd make even greater strides with an impressive series of roles.

Before discussing her big year in 1988, it's worth noting that prior to 1987 Pfeiffer appeared in several telefilms. In 1981 alone she made *Splendor in the Grass*, *Callie and Son* and *The Children Nobody Wanted*. In 1985 her *ABC Afterschool Special*

episode *One Too Many* paired her up with another rising star, Val Kilmer. In November of 1987, just a few months after *The Witches of Eastwick* had raised her profile, she starred in a feature-length episode of the *Great Performances* series, alternately titled *Tales from the Hollywood Hills: Natica Jackson* and *Power, Passion and Murder*. It would be the last time she appeared in a television production that decade, and she would rarely return to the medium until recent years. That's because by 1988 her movie career truly elevated to the next level.

Pfeiffer's banner year in 1988 allowed her to show off her range as an actress with three very different roles in three vastly different films. In hindsight, she had an astonishing year, the kind most actors dream of but never achieve. The first of the three Pfeiffer films released that year *Married to the Mob* (1988) opened in August, with *Tequila Sunrise* (1988) dropping in early December and *Dangerous Liaisons* (1988) premiering at the end of the year, just in time to qualify for that year's Academy Awards - and Pfeiffer would benefit

from that timing. But first, she began her stellar year with the starring role in a New York City mob comedy that would afford her the chance to display her broad range as an actress, while carrying a film as the lead.

Jonathan Demme's *Married to the Mob* is wonderfully eccentric, refreshingly sweet, and a perfect starring vehicle for Pfeiffer. The role of Angela de Marco, conflicted Long Island mafia widow, allows her to express the breadth of her range, from comedy to drama, and she delivers magnificently. Angela is emancipating herself and her young son from a life she doesn't want by forging a new, mob-free existence for the two of them in New York City. Of course, the mob won't let her go that easily. Neither will the FBI.

Everything in the film revolves around Angela, and at this point in her career Pfeiffer proves she's more than capable of carrying the film on her slim shoulders. Demme recognized that her gift for facial expressions is an important part of her acting prowess. He clearly knew what he had in Pfeiffer's face and, most importantly, he knew what to

do with it. Throughout, the director's camera frames her beautifully, in one dazzling closeup after another. That remarkable, expressive face shows us Angela's journey from kept mafia wife to independent single mom. The closeups are extraordinarily powerful, thanks to her talent for conveying emotions with just a look. Her eyes are a veritable barometer of Angela's heart and soul, filling with pain, anger, and tears as her mob husband (Alec Baldwin) laughs off her demands for a divorce. Later, those calm, reassuring eyes soothe her son's distress after his father's death. When she falls for the undercover FBI agent who's trailing her (Matthew Modine), her eyes practically sparkle like diamonds, and her big, bright smile offers pure cinematic bliss. Pfeiffer and Modine possess an easy, natural chemistry and together infuse the film with a sweet and touching central romance. *Married to the Mob* is an achingly beautiful film, and Pfeiffer's performance is a huge reason why.

Sandwiched between her two exquisite 1988 performances in *Married to the Mob* and *Dangerous Liaisons* resides the neo-noir *Tequila Sunrise*. Directed by Robert Towne, starring Mel Gibson and Kurt Russell, and featuring Pfeiffer in a third wheel/girlfriend role, it's easy to forget this film when considering Pfeiffer's best, but it remains an underrated entry. Gibson plays 'Mac' McKussic, a conflicted drug dealer with a Mexican connection. He's also a sensitive single dad raising a young son in a California beach town. Kurt Russell is his old friend Nick Frescia, a police lieutenant hot on the trail of his buddy's criminal activity. Pfeiffer rounds out the main trio as Jo Ann (Giovanna) Vallenari, owner and manager of Vallenari's Italian restaurant, where Mac can be found most nights dining on her delicious Rigatoni ai Quattro Formaggi - and getting lost in her beautiful blue eyes.

Towne apparently clashed with Pfeiffer over her acting style and choices, with the writer-director later complaining that she was the most difficult actress he'd ever worked with. Hopefully she takes that as a badge of honor. It is precisely what caused Towne headaches that makes the performance so good. Her acting style is more organic and intuitive than a controlling director might prefer. She feels the part deeply, and builds off the script in ways that transcend literal interpretation. From the moment we first meet Jo Ann in the restaurant, she feels authentic. The only woman with a substantial role in the cast, she doesn't just "hold her own with the boys," as '80s audiences might have put it. No, instead she simply

delivers an utterly compelling performance, while making it look easy. We know she put in the work, but it comes off as effortlessly real. It's quintessential Pfeiffer.

She closed out her extraordinary year in 1988 with an Oscar-nominated supporting role in Stephen Frears' eighteenth-century period piece *Dangerous Liaisons*. It was the first time the Academy recognized Pfeiffer's work and it marked a turning point in her career. Before *Dangerous Liaisons* she was a rising talent, garnering good reviews but not yet considered an upper echelon actress. While I would argue that Oscar nominations and wins are mostly meaningless, there's no denying it can prove to be a career booster. Her first Oscar nod moved her into an elite category of actresses, and over the following four years she would earn two more Oscar nominations, both for Best Actress. She also turned in two other career-best performances during that span that didn't even get nominated (I'm looking at you, Frankie from *Frankie and Johnny* [1991] and you too, Selina Kyle from *Batman Returns* [1992]).

Her performance as Madame Marie de Tourvel in *Dangerous Liaisons* is simply majestic. She strikes one sublime note after another as a tragic woman of virtue whose emotions are maliciously toyed with by two

duplicitous characters, played by John Malkovich and Glenn Close. Pfeiffer brings a striking innocence to the role, which makes her tour-de-force scene such a revelation. When Malkovich's Valmont cruelly breaks her heart, Marie's composure collapses under a torrent of tears as Pfeiffer makes evident Marie's heartache and devastation. Roger Ebert praised her performance, noting that: "In a year that has seen her in varied assignments such as *Married to the Mob* and *Tequila Sunrise*, the movie is more evidence of her versatility. She is good when she is innocent and superb when she is guilty."

After this breakout year in 1988, what could Pfeiffer possibly do to top it? Only turn in what might be her signature performance in writer-director Steve Kloves' lovely, melancholic *The Fabulous Baker Boys*, for which she earned her second straight Oscar nomination, this time for Best Actress. From her memorable introduction, stumbling into frame on a broken heel while cursing aloud, all the way through to the film's sweet and hopeful final scene, Pfeiffer is a triumph throughout. As the cynical, sarcastic former call girl Susie Diamond, she reveals how Susie's cynicism acts as her protection against fear and failure. With this role, everything she had been working towards as an actress in the '80s was fully realized.

Susie joins the piano-playing lounge act The Fabulous Baker Boys and shakes up the personal and professional lives of brothers Frank and Jack Baker (real life brothers Beau and Jeff Bridges, respectively). Seven years after singing *Cool Rider* and other songs in *Grease 2*, Pfeiffer would once more lay down her own vocals, including *More Than You Know* and *Makin' Whoopee*. Both performances are showstoppers. *More Than You Know* serves as Susie's audition for the Baker Boys and it's a prophetic song choice, as we quickly learn there is more to Susie than meets the eye. She's wearing a micro-miniskirt and heels, aggressively chewing gum and wisecracking about the low-rent stakes of this audition - "*This* is show business?" Yet once she begins to sing her achingly vulnerable

rendition, the Baker brothers and the audience realize she also possesses a lovely singing voice and an undeniable magnetism as a performer. This charisma shines onstage throughout, but most especially in the iconic New Year's Eve performance of *Makin' Whoopee*. The lyrics, her sultry vocal delivery, and the way she seductively climbs atop Jack's piano during the song combine for a truly indelible movie moment. Even if you haven't seen *The Fabulous Baker Boys*, you *know* the *Makin' Whoopee* scene.

Once again, Ebert found the right words when he correctly noted: "This is one of the movies they will use as a document, years from now, when they begin to trace the steps by which Pfeiffer became a great star." It's true, and Susie was, at that point in Pfeiffer's career, the role of a lifetime. Smartly written by Kloves, Susie has some terrifically funny dialogue, like: "Listen, you're not going soft on me, are you? I mean, you're not going to start dreaming about me and waking up all sweaty and looking at me like I'm some sort of princess when I burp?" Susie's words are also keenly perceptive and brutally honest: "And you kid yourself that you've got this empty place inside where you can put it all. But you do it long enough and all you are is empty." As well written as the role might be, it's Pfeiffer who manages to make Susie into a fully dimensional person of great depth and heart. Even though she was clearly the obvious choice for the

For 31 years it's been just the Fabulous Baker Boys...

...but times change.

jeff bridges · michelle pfeiffer · beau bridges
the fabulous baker boys

GLADDEN ENTERTAINMENT Presents A MIRAGE PRODUCTION JEFF BRIDGES MICHELLE PFEIFFER BEAU BRIDGES
THE FABULOUS BAKER BOYS Executive Music Producer JOEL SILL Music by DAVE GRUSIN Edited by WILLIAM STEINKAMP
Production Designer JEFFREY TOWNSEND Director of Photography MICHAEL BALLHAUS, A.S.C. Co-Producer BILL FINNEGAN
Executive Producer SYDNEY POLLACK Produced by PAULA WEINSTEIN and MARK ROSENBERG
Written and Directed by STEVE KLOVES
Soundtrack Available On GRP CD's Cassettes and Records.

Academy Award for Best Actress that year, the Academy missed the mark once again and she went home without an Oscar. It's particularly galling, considering she swept most other major awards, including the Golden Globes, British Academy Film Awards and National Society of Film Critics, among many others. Ultimately, whether she won an Oscar for *The Fabulous Baker Boys* doesn't matter. The performance speaks for itself and has done so brilliantly for close to thirty-five years now.

After ending the '80s on an extraordinary high, Pfeiffer steamrolled into the '90s as one of the top actresses in Hollywood, a position she has held now for the last three decades. She's taken some breaks from acting to spend time with her family, yet she's always returned and remains as in-demand as ever. In recent years she's become a recurring member of the Marvel Cinematic Universe in the *Ant-Man* movies while also crafting exquisite performances in independent films like *French Exit* (2020). She's both a fan favorite and a critical darling, and it was in the '80s that she first established what makes her such a special talent: a natural, utterly believable acting style and a memorably charismatic screen presence. One need only look at some of her best '80s work, like Elvira in *Scarface*, Angela in *Married to the Mob*, Marie in *Dangerous Liaisons* or Susie in *The Fabulous Baker Boys* to see that her enormous talent was already burning bright during the first decade of her career. It was a decade of ascension for Pfeiffer, and in her wake she left behind indelible cinematic performances that continue to resonate today.

LEWIS COLLINS - THE MACARONI COMBAT YEARS

by Ian Talbot Taylor

In Issue 1 of 'Cinema of the '80s', I charted the rise of Lewis Collins from hairdresser to '60s beat group musician, from television light comedy actor to action man and finally big budget star of the Euan Lloyd production *Who Dares Wins* (US title *The Final Option*). Things were looking bright for Lew, with a meeting concerning the James Bond role and more Lloyd productions promised. So, how did Mr. Collins end up in the Philippines working for the Italian director Antonio Margheriti?

Well, the simple fact is that the actor was kicking his heels waiting for movement on the next Lloyd productions, including *Wild Geese 2*. His popularity in Europe was still high thanks to broadcasts of *The Professionals* television series and he was therefore offered a three-picture deal to headline Italian/German-funded war films directed by Margheriti. Some sources claim that Collins was fired from *Wild Geese 2* by a furious Lloyd when the first Margheriti title was changed from *Codename: Commando* or *Commando Force* to *Codename: Wild Geese* in order to capitalise on the success of the *The Wild Geese* and *The Soldier* (aka *Codename: The Soldier* in Europe). Apparently, some would have it that Lloyd wanted no mistaken connection between his planned sequel and a European rip-off and so dropped Collins. Other sources suggest that Lloyd simply felt he needed a different actor/ character to avoid confusion with *Who Dares Wins* and so recast *Wild Geese 2* with Scott Glenn. The other planned projects simply fizzled out. Either way, Collins ended up in a dubbed, Asian-set combat zone, and whilst these productions didn't get cinema releases in the UK, they certainly earned a few rentals on the VHS market.

Not that he was overly impressed with his own vehicles. "They were crap films, and I only did them for the money," said Collins later. Of course, a cheque's a cheque. And at least he got to work with some genuine big-name stars, even if they might have been past their prime.

Basically, *Codename: Wild Geese* (1984) is exactly what one might expect from a macaroni combat movie. There is plenty of action, good use of exotic (if cheap) locations and ropey dialogue. Naturally, a popular British or American name heads the cast. It's Collins here, but other similar productions had made use of David Warbeck (*The Beyond*), Oliver Tobias (*The Stud*) and Richard Hatch (*Battlestar Galactica*). What is impressive in this case is the co-stars. Collins is joined by Lee Van Cleef and Ernest Borgnine of Hollywood fame, and Klaus Kinski, Mimsy Farmer, Manfred Lehmann and Luciano Pigozzi who were all busy European performers.

The film opens with one of those very '80s synthesiser scores which make one long for the bombast of full orchestral soundtracks of yesteryear. Still, Margheriti hits the ground running, taking our minds off the plinks and plonks of the music. The opening scene is immediately dramatic with choppers soaring above the jungles of the Philippines. Down on the ground, Collins as mercenary Commander Robin Wesley leads his team through the thick foliage and makes tense facial expressions and those cool hand signals that soldiers always make. Sometimes, Lewis gets a bad rap as an actor but he's just as screen-friendly as he was when he became a television darling in the UK during the '70s.

Meanwhile, Margheriti does his bit on the other side of

the camera, excelling at directing action sequences. The opening approach on an enemy base is first tense, then high-octane fun, making the most of hoary old favourites such as crawling through a minefield and slow-motion explosions and extras flying gracefully through the air. There are also some dramatic and exotic locations, with lovely long shots.

True, the characterisations are borderline caricature, the scripted cyphers are paper thin and obvious, but no-one watches an Italian war rip-off for deep messages and soul-searching performances. Collins plays Wesley as a well-spoken officer type, but he's still hard as nails (convincingly so, as we might expect from an actor who trained with the SAS for real). Some of the things he does might be comparable to Bodie in *The Professionals* or Skellen in *Who Dares Wins* but he is a notably different character.

The script clearly riffs off *The Wild Geese* and James Bond. Wesley has become a mercenary as a means of numbing the pain of losing his son to drugs. He gets his orders from a suited and booted boss in a hi-tech office block, the exposition a mere MacGuffin to get our hero into the mix.

Kinski plays Charlton, a snide and smarmy contact who,

one always suspects, is up to no good in his 'Man from Del Monte' white suit and shades. Borgnine is a US official supposedly, but of course, Borgnine is Borgnine in the most perfect way. Sadly, this is only a glorified cameo, but no film is worse for his presence and it's lovely to see Lewis Collins of TV fame playing opposite a genuine Oscar winner. Van Cleef at least gets more to do as a military prisoner turned pilot hero (they're even chucking *The Dirty Dozen* into it!) I could continue to tick off the cribs from other, often bigger movies. *The Wild Geese* has been referenced plenty already, but there are other clear steals such as the team radioing desperately from hostile territory and getting screwed by their own bosses. The obvious lift is emphasised further by the use of a 'Wild Geese' call sign! The vengeful coda is also very, very familiar though I'll not describe it in case a) you have not seen the film yet, and b) you can't work out the bleedin' obvious! Elsewhere, there are Bond style car tricks - all obvious small-scale model work in this case, but still reasonably passable - and Borgnine's face during this is priceless. Finally, one of the sequences filmed in Hong Kong possibly uses the same hilltop restaurant location utilised by Hammer Films for the relatively obscure thriller *Shatter* (1974) starring Stuart Whitman and Peter Cushing. Nevertheless, we must accept that everybody knew what game the filmmakers were playing. These productions are created to cash in on better known films. Where they shine most is in their crazily enthusiastic action sequences that ask stuntmen to go further than is good for them! Margheriti knows how to create atmosphere through setting and then light the blue touch paper. And the introduction of an old, ruined church in the jungle, presided over by an uncredited Pigozzi is pure Italian multi-genre magnificence, especially the massacre that ensues, culminating in his crucifixion. Shocking, emotive, tragic, backed with a religious slant to the score by Jan Nemec. In scenes like this, *Codename: Wild Geese* presents its unique identity. Considered as a whole though, this is a cocktail of gunfire, conflagrations, intrigue and stern facial expressions. Sometimes, that's all you need.

Collins began 1985 with only the next Margheriti picture to look forward to. Television-wise, he was still visible through repeats of *The Professionals*, but this perhaps proved to cause typecasting issues. A notable exception was his gloriously camp interpretation of the Sheriff of Nottingham in an episode of ITV drama *Robin of Sherwood*. And although it didn't involve performance nor payment for Lewis, he was beautifully and hilariously celebrated in children's TV show *Fat Tulip's Garden* through the inclusion of a stunt tortoise named Lewis Collins who would always wear a crash helmet and attempt daredevil feats. Collins had a sense of humour. He could take that.

When Margheriti's *Commando Leopard* arrived, there were times when viewers might surely feel that they were watching the preceding film still. As well as Collins, there were returns from Kinski, Pigozzi, Manfred Lehmann and Thomas Danneberg and many of the locations looked as if (and could well have been) the very same places, despite the story being set in South America this time! The filming actually took place in the Philippines and Venezuela.

Marking the changes as Margheriti dives straight into the action, it transpires that a stubbled Collins is now a legendary rebel by the name of Enrique Carrasco. The addition of pan pipes to the score (a cheap way of establishing a setting!) elevates it, and how can pan pipes sound dramatic? Who knows, but they do!

There was Swiss finance behind it (an estimated 15 million Swiss Francs made it the most expensive Swiss-budgeted movie at that point). Clearly, most of this went on admittedly excellent miniature model work. There is a wonderful dam location and it's special effects destruction is absolutely magnificent, as is the similar demise of a pontoon bridge. The action is also better choreographed, with yet another uneasy atmosphere draped over a church-cum-hospital full of injured bodies and displaced villagers. There is a tangible sense of pathos, an unshakeable understanding that not all of the good guys will make it out alive, and a very Italian brutality.

Collins is absolutely the best hero, Kinski is the baddest villain and Lehmann the most tragic character, and just when the movie seems to reach a natural end, we get an extra ten minutes off explosive action with Collins riding to the rescue atop a jeep.

The director plots the fight sequences well amongst claustrophobically grouped ruins and old buildings. Eventually, the downtrodden turn against the dictator, the power of the cross plays its part (though not dishonestly so) and the whole shebang comes to a close with genuine emotional impact. Sold to around 100 countries after the reasonable financial success of *Codename: Wild Geese*, *Commando Leopard* may not reach Hollywood levels, but it reaches for the stars as an international film and comes darned close at times.

The 2005 Anchor Bay UK DVD release features an intriguing 49-minutes documentary featuring behind the scenes shots of Collins practising scenes without a gun, then performing for real and then gooning around afterwards. It really highlights his character: convincingly tough but fun. Taking it seriously but as light as anything afterwards. This contrasts with Kinski's temper - shouting and scowling when an extra mistimes a move.

"Take another one, that's shit!"

Lehmann looks uncomfortable with the histrionics but when Kinksi is interviewed, he puts it down to impatience with rehearsals or multiple takes. He is more focused on showing off his beautiful girlfriend or posing in front of a mirror pre-take.

When producer Erwin C Dietrich is asked about the two contrasting actors, he replies: "Every actor gets out of (Kinski's) way… last time he had his problems with Ernest Borgnine, now he has his problems with Collins… this is Kinski."

A smirking Lewis quips: "I haven't worked with Kinski in close proximity. I find him very interesting, if not unusual… obviously there are lots of stories around Klaus, he's got his own charisma and so on. I think a lot of it's self-generated, but he's good and that's the main thing."

When asked if Collins thinks Kinski likes him, he replies: "No idea. He hasn't kissed me yet."

Collins comes across exceedingly well in behind-the-scenes footage, listening seriously to Margheiti whilst still having a laugh. He talks self-deprecatingly about his former

life as failed "rock and pop star", deflects questions about Bond and suggests his dream role would be producer/ director. It's gratifying to see him maintain his sense of humour when the interview is interrupted by banging, when the camera spies on his script-reading or when he's in the make-up chair.

Intriguingly, he also mentions heading to America for something like *Jaws* but with rattlesnakes and a couple of non-action films that fell through. He was looking more towards straight theatre, believing it to be 'proper acting' and film/TV being just for the financial success.

In February 1987, Collins witnessed a road accident involving two young girls. He and his cousin offered assistance when one girl struggled to breathe. Lewis pressed her head back and managed to get her breathing again. His cousin claimed that "she might have died if he hadn't been so quick".

This was obviously a great thing, but it ironically continued to feed the 'action man' stereotype. Collins reflected that "the British public have an image of me that I'm not sure I can escape... I was an action man all my life, even before I became an actor. I was a champion rifle shot at the age of 14, a judo expert, rode motorbikes, yet people say I am living out the art of Bodie".

He had a bit-part in US TV-film *Carly's Web* (1987) but then it was back to all that action with his final Margheriti jungle warfare picture - *The Commander*, which began shooting in October 1987.

Shot in the Philippines, Thailand, Italy and Germany, this movie (released in 1988) offers yet mor impressive scenery but really feels like a throwback, with casting, locations and situations mirroring *Codename: Wild Geese*. Van Cleef returns, as a baddie this time, as does John Steiner from *Commando Leopard* and Lehmann and Danneberg who both complete a hattrick by appearing in the entire loose trilogy. Collins is a mercenary again (this time Major Colby in camouflage and red beret) and he battles against corruption, Asian military and a synth-heavy score by Eloy.

As expected by now, the director orchestrates a well-choreographed opening manoeuvre featuring impressive moves, explosions and hardware, but there is now too much gangster-ish to-ing and fro-ing between various factions. Donald Pleasence has fun as a growlingly mischievous, cigar-smoking American Ambassador surrounded by 'yes men', but Brett Halsey barely makes a mark amongst the internecine shenanigans. Meanwhile Bobby (*Demons*) Rhodes has the most annoyingly fake laugh on display, but at least strikes a charismatic figure.

Van Cleef does a bit of poisoning, Collins does a bit of *Dirty Dozen/Magnificent Seven*-type teambuilding, but for a movie that, like its predecessors, banks on its action sequences, this is a slow-moving tale, lacking money shots. Some ill-matched footage of military helicopters from elsewhere really shows that *The Commander* lacks the budget of the previous two pictures. In fact, some sequences are nicked from *Codename: Wild Geese* -

ERWIN C. DIETRICH
PRESENTS

LEWIS COLLINS
LEE VAN CLEEF
DONALD PLEASANCE

LEWIS COLLINS

LEE VAN CLEEF

DONALD PLEASANCE

CHAT SILAYAN

THE COMMANDER

THE ASCOT FILM CORPORATION PRESENTS A ANTHONY M. DAWSON FILM
LEWIS COLLINS · LEE VAN CLEEF · DONALD PLEASANCE · JOHN STEINER
MANFRED LEHMAN · BRETT HALSEY · CHAT SILAYAN · BOBBY RHODES · TOM DANNEBERG · PAUL MULLER
FRANK GLAUBRECHT · ROMANO PUPPO · HANS LEUTENEGGER
WRITTEN BY ARNE ELSHOLTZ AND TITO CARPI PRODUCED BY ERWIN C. DIETRICH DIRECTOR OF PHOTOGRAPHY PETER BAUMGARTNER
DIRECTED BY ANTHONY M. DAWSON

recognise that silo? You should! It could also do without the cockfighting sequence, but then Italian exploitation cinema has historically had problems regarding animal welfare, of course.

Fair play, there is a bunch of gunfighting just on the hour mark, with a bit of grenade lobbing even a bit of mud wrestling (!) between Lehmann and Steiner. There is some tension on a river journey leading to the villainous General Dong, and late ambiguity regarding Major Colby's motives is stirred up.

Collins looks very tired by this point, with bags under the bags that are under his eyes, and I doubt it was down to make-up.

There is a fair bit of action in the final 20 minutes, though some of it is archive material. Collins and Lehmann's character mistrust each other almost to the end but finally acquiesce to an agreement which allows them to smoke out the manipulative villain of the piece. It's no spoiler to name Van Cleef as the major bad guy - it was really no great secret.

Overall, *The Commander* is disappointing because the progress made from *Codename: Wild Geese* to *Commando Leopard* seems to have slipped through the team's fingers. It was no surprise that this marked the end of Collins' working relationship with producer Dietrich and director Margheriti.

Things looked up for Collins that same year when he was hired to play buddy cop to Michael Caine's Inspector Abberline in David Wickes' superior TV mini-series *Jack the Ripper*. As had always really been the case, it was the small screen in the living room that was Collins' bread and butter. For a while, work continued to come in steadily. A role in the German crime drama *Blue Blood* and an episode of the updated *Alfred Hitchcock Presents* (both 1989), a role alongside names like Oliver Reed, Sarah Miles and Christopher Plummer in a TV-movie adaption of Barbara

Cartland's historical romance *A Ghost in Monte Carlo* (1990) and short runs in series such as *Cluedo* and *The Grimleys* in the UK and a France/Canada/Mexico adaption of *Tarzan*. Lewis made his final dramatic role on-screen in an episode of British police soap opera (they like to call them ongoing serials these days) *The Bill* in 2002.

Lewis Collins gave up on acting and relocated to America where he lived with his wife and children whilst selling computers for a living. He took film directing courses and at one point was in talks to star in a sequel series to *The Professionals* wherein he would revive the character of William Arthur Phillip Bodie, now the boss of CI5 as a replacement for Gordon Jackson's Cowley. Collins' confident obstinacy seemed to have reared its head as he was eventually jettisoned from negotiations and Edward Woodward was hired to play a completely different character instead. The show bombed and was canned after one series.

In early 2012, his agents announced Lewis' return to acting. He been cast to play the role of the Earl Godwin in the historical drama film *1066*. Sadly, in June 2013, it was announced that he had withdrawn from the production due to ill health. Collins had been first diagnosed with cancer in 2008, and tragically died at the age of 67 in Los Angeles on 27 November 2013.

For an actor often underestimated, he had a commendable run of success, but for the promise he showed, he was massively unfortunate not to catch the breaks that would have established him as a worldwide superstar.

His macaroni combat trilogy are hardly the heights of cinema, but they provide a fascinating showcase of a man who didn't just act the role but could truly live the life for real. Lewis Collins, less known in the USA, a familiar and likeable star in the UK and Europe, was the tough yet genial real deal.

by Kevin Nickelson

Oscar Wilde once said: "Imitation is the sincerest form of flattery." It's a mantra which has kept film executives flush in Rolls Royces, luxurious swimming pools and yearly trips to the French Riviera. It has also satiated the fanaticism of many a movie viewer. The '80s, for example, saw a boom in a niche cinematic genre called "sword and sorcery", which largely imitated the sword and sandal cycle, throwing in the sort of fantasy elements (wizards, witches, demons, etc.) one would expect to find in a Harryhausen *Sinbad* film. Many sword and sorcery movies culled their ideas from a collection of Middle Eastern folk tales named 'Arabian Nights: One Thousand and One Nights'.

The formula really blossomed in cinematic terms when stop-motion effects pioneer Ray Harryhausen gave young fans the gleeful classic *The 7th Voyage of Sinbad* (1958) and the epic *Jason and the Argonauts* (1963). In the literary world, the genre was championed by authors like Andre Norton (the *nom de plume* of Alice Mary Norton) who wrote book series such as 'The Cycle of Oak, Yew, Ash, and Rowan' (2000-2005) and 'Carolus Rex' (begun in 1999). The 'Hosteen Storm/Beast Master' series, launched by her in 1959, is what Norton is perhaps best remembered for nowadays, thanks largely to the 1982 screen adaptation co-written and directed by Don Coscarelli and starring Marc Singer, Tanya Roberts and Rip Torn.

After the modest box office success of *Hawk the Slayer* (1980) and *Dragonslayer* (1981), 1982 saw a real surge in gleaming steel adventure-fantasy projects. The likes of pulp spectacular *Conan the Barbarian*, Joe D'Amato's highly

fun *Ator the Fighting Eagle* and Albert Pyun's wild *The Sword and the Sorcerer* all shone prominently for many weeks on the marquee boards of that year. Ever the enterprising talents, Coscarelli and fellow writer Paul Pepperman came up with a fantasy movie script of their own, loosely based on Norton's novel. They eschewed much of what Norton had put on the literary page, reworking the Navajo-inspired hero Hosteen Storm into a Conan-esque character named Dar and transforming the futuristic sci-fi setting into a pseudo-Robert E. Howard land of kings and warlocks. The hero's telepathic connection with the wildlife was virtually the only element from the book to make it into the finished script.

The story in the film version concerns Dar (Singer) growing up among a tribe, unaware that he is the son of an imprisoned king. He was spirited away as a baby after being marked for death by the power-crazed warlock, Maax (Torn), who fears a prophecy predicting his eventual downfall at Dar's hands. Dar has a strange gift which enables him to communicate with animals. After his adopted tribe are wiped out by Maax's army, Dar sets off for revenge, picking up a panther, two ferrets and a hawk as companions along the way. After befriending a slave girl named Kiri (Roberts) who is destined to be sacrificed, Dar learns about his true past. He discovers his real father is still alive, albeit guarded in an impenetrable fortress. He vows to lead a rebellion against Maax and his followers to free the land from their reign of terror.

Norton, in an interview with 'Starlog' magazine in 1989, revealed her total dismay with the production: "I thought it was *dreadful. Awful.* I made them remove my name from any connection with it the moment I read the script and saw that it bore *no* resemblance to my book! And did you know that the poor tiger they used in that movie *died* because they had to tranquilize it to dye it black, and it had a reaction to the drug? I was very upset when I heard that! You see, my agent sold the movie rights, but I didn't have script approval. So, they made a movie that had *nothing* to do with my book." Asked if there had been further attempts to translate her books to the screen, Norton seemed to evoke the old saying "Fool me once, shame on you; fool me twice, shame on *me*." She remarked: "There has been discussion, but I won't let anything else go unless I have script approval, and they don't like to give that to the author."

But if you accept the film as another entry in the then-trendy sword and sorcery cycle rather than an adaptation of Norton's literature, then it contains many exciting if silly elements which coalesce nicely in the finished product. It's surprising to learn how many problems came up during filming. For one, the producer-director relationship was quite strained at times, as indicated by Coscarelli and executive producer Sylvio Tabet in several interviews. Donald Guarisco of Schlockmania spoke to Tabet about his difficult relationship with Coscarelli, but Tabet told him: "I consider Don a very talented director and there is no reason we cannot work together again." He lamented the $9 million budget of *The Beastmaster*, though, saying: "I come from commercials. I shot nearly 400 hundred of them. Most were shot in Lebanon where budgets were very tight. I had sets built strictly to capture the angle of the lenses we were using."

Coscarelli and Tabet also disagreed over who to cast in the role of main female character, Kiri. The director wanted Demi Moore but Tabet overruled him in favor of Roberts. Either would have been suitable to be honest, as the part mainly calls for someone young and statuesque who can carry off the skimpy costumes and physical action. There were also plenty of arguments over the editing. The original 1982 theatrical cut (the same version used in Vinegar Syndrome's 2021 4K Ultra HD set) runs at 118 minutes, but a 90-minute version was released in Europe for the VHS release. That's a huge difference in running times, and it gives a clear idea of the harshness of the post-production editing which took place. Coscarelli stated a certain disdain for the longer cut. When asked if a director's cut was in the works, he told IGN: "Unfortunately a lot of the material we shot is lost and gone. No, there is no director's cut. If I was to make a director's cut, it would be a lot shorter. The 120-minute version I think could be 10 or 15 minutes shorter." Nonetheless, it would still be a good 20 minutes longer than the ruthlessly hacked 90-minute VHS version.

Like Norton said, there was an infamous case of animal

abuse attached to the film. The producers decided that a tiger should be used during the panther sequences in the story, since they'd been told tigers were easier to handle than panthers. It was necessary to have the tigers dyed black, which required each to be tranquilized first. An erroneous rumor went around that one of the cats died two years later due to toxicity of the chemicals in the dye. It's true that Sultan, one of the tigers, passed away two years later, but this was proven to have been caused by a bad reaction to the drug contained in the tranquilizer, which had a long-term impact on the creature's health. Coscarelli referred to the incident in an interview with author Staci Layne Wilson for her 2007 book 'Animal Movies Guide'. He explained the dye was of a non-toxic black vegetable variety which caused no harm to the tiger. The tranquilizer, however, contained chemicals which triggered unforeseen health problems for the big cat. Coscarelli has expressed numerous times how horrible he felt about its death and that it was a tragedy no-one could have predicted.

What makes *The Beastmaster* truly shine for me are its truly stunning visuals, the sheer charisma and energy of its stars, and the plentiful action set-pieces. Location shooting took place in California's Simi Valley, Los Padres National Forest's Lake Piru in Ventura County and Valley of Fire State Park in Nevada. These backdrops frame the

tale gloriously, helped by the expert eye of esteemed cinematographer John Alcott. Marc Singer spoke to Karen Beishuizen of Ringside Report recently and said his two fondest memories of working on the film were the physicality of the role and the chance to watch Alcott gloriously capturing the vistas. "As a student of kung fu at the Seattle Kung Fu Club under the guidance of Grand Master John S.S. Leong, I had a pretty good sense of swordplay and - largely thanks to that training and a constitution strong enough to stand up to the rigors of filming in all sorts of weather - I held my own in the stunts. The stunt community, as I'm sure people are aware, is comprised of very sturdy individuals, and they appreciated my efforts to contribute as much as I appreciated their generosity in encouraging me to participate. I learned a lot about filmmaking from them, and from the Academy Award-winning director of photography John Alcott."

Roberts landed the role of Kiri thanks to the insistence of the producer. She told James Verniere of 'Fangoria' in 1983: "I accepted *The Beastmaster* because it gave me the chance to slip into movies without getting the whole book thrown at me. The movie wasn't built around me. I was just an actor in it, and it was a good chance for me to be seen." Filmgoers get quite an intimate view of her as it happens, in a scene where the actress appears topless in a pool after Dar's mischievous ferrets steal her garments. "Oh, it's such a short shot that you don't even notice it", she told Verniere. "Please, tell me you didn't notice it?!

I was so embarrassed. The crew was supposed to take a hike while we shot it, but I know there were fifty guys hiding in the bushes! You know what crews are like!"

Supporting Singer and Roberts are stellar veterans who bring considerable TV and film experience to the movie. John Amos, of *Good Times* and *Roots* fame, plays Dar's warrior friend Seth. And the scene-stealing Rip Torn portrays the villainous Maax (a role originally meant for Klaus Kinski). Coscarelli had a very amusing meeting with Torn at the start. "He came to the film with his own peculiar ideas about how the character was going to be played," said the director. "He came to me and said: 'I want to play this role like a turkey vulture.'" It was Torn himself who supplied the beaked fake nose his character sports throughout.

The Beastmaster enjoyed only modest initial success, accumulating some $14.1 million on release. It has,

however, grown to near cult status in the years since. The significance of the film on both a personal level as well as in its cultural legacy was not lost on Singer. He told Tara Rice of 'Magic Image Hollywood': "*The Beastmaster* was significant to me in a whole lot of ways… There I was in my own life walking around with a 450lb Bengal tiger, and then the film itself was very successful, almost in its own way cultishly iconic… Perhaps the best explanation as to why it remains in the minds and hearts of fans is its near-metaphysical kismet."

It's true to say the film has a dedicated fan base to this day. It might not be an accurate translation of the book to screen, but it is an entertaining sword and sorcery offering with much to enjoy.

Mark L. Lester
Interview

With just four films in the '80s, Mark L. Lester reinvented the action film, upset film censors, adapted Stephen King, and worked with John Candy and Meg Ryan.

David Michael Brown chats to the filmmaker about his most successful decade behind the camera…

DMB: Was *Class of 1984* (1982) influenced by your own school days? Watching the film, I hope not.

ML: Yes, unfortunately, it was. There was a gang at my high school, Monroe High School in San Fernando Valley, and I got beaten up. It was not as extreme as in the film, but they had knives and would steal your lunch. When I returned to my old

The teachers at Lincoln High have a very dangerous problem… their students!

A MARK LESTER Film
CLASS OF 1984

CLASS OF 1984
Starring PERRY KING · MERRIE LYNN ROSS · TIMOTHY VAN PATTEN
STEFAN ARNGRIM · MICHAEL FOX and RODDY McDOWALL as Corrigan
Director of Photography ALBERT DUNK, A.S.C. · Music by LALO SCHIFRIN
Song "I AM THE FUTURE" performed by ALICE COOPER
Screenplay by MARK LESTER and JOHN SAXTON and TOM HOLLAND · Story by TOM HOLLAND
Executive Producers MARK LESTER and MERRIE LYNN ROSS · Produced by ARTHUR KENT
Directed by MARK LESTER
Released by UNITED FILM DISTRIBUTION COMPANY · R

high school years later, I was shocked to discover how degenerated it had become. Gangs were roaming the school corridors; graffiti was sprayed on the walls and kids were fighting in the hallways. And I thought, wow, this is not like when I went to high school, so I researched all these incidents. And there was a teacher who brought a gun to a classroom. So that became a scene in the movie. It's my favourite movie I've made

because of where it came from. I was inspired by *Blackboard Jungle* (1955) which I saw as a kid. I also wanted to pay homage to the gang mentality of *A Clockwork Orange* (1971).

DMB: *Class of 1984* is known for its punk aesthetic and soundtrack…

ML: I was reading British magazines. I loved the punk style of dress, the Mohawks, and the attitude. It was anarchy. *Class of 1984* was the first

US movie really to showcase the whole punk rock style. They were sticking pins into themselves, slam-dancing and pogoing and spitting at the shows. For the scene in that punk club, I advertised for real punk rockers. And I interviewed every extra myself. They were real punkers. And when they came into that club, they were so wild. We had various local punk groups playing on set. The whole scene was exhilarating to be part of.

DMB: You mentioned the music. How important was it was it for you to get the music right for the film?

ML: Very! I never thought I'd get Lalo Schifrin to do something like this, but he was very adventurous and liked to step out of his comfort zone. His movie scores were not for movies like this. But he wanted to stay with the times to keep current. So, I got him. This was the Lalo Schifrin who wrote the scores for *Cool Hand Luke* (1967) and *Dirty Harry* (1971)! I also contacted a punk rock label here in Los Angeles for the punk rock cuts in the movie.

DMB: You also got Alice Cooper singing the theme tune?

ML: It was Lalo's idea to get Alice Cooper for the title song. When we scheduled Alice to record the song, he was meant to arrive at the studio at 9:00am, but he showed up at 9:00pm! All day long cases of vodka were arriving, but not Alice. But he finally arrived, and he did a great job. I am the future, and nothing can stop us. Right? And that, again, is very prophetic because nothing has stopped crazy people in high schools.

DMB: Can you talk about casting *Class of 1984*?

ML: I was a fan of Perry King in Andy Warhol's *Bad* (1975) and then *Mandingo* (1977). He was young then, like 30-something, so I was interested in getting him to do it. And he was fantastic in the film. And there's a funny moment in *Class of 1984* where he had to cut this guy's arm off with a circular saw. He said: "this is too gross. I don't want to do it. I don't want to do it. I'm not cutting this guy's arm off." I said: "Perry, you abused slaves

in *Mandingo*. That was pretty bad. And a baby was thrown out of a window in Bad. I think you're OK with an arm?" [*Laughs*] "Oh, you're right, Mark. I'll do it!".

DMB: And Timothy Van Patten is fantastic in the bad guy role...

ML: He is! Timothy was on a TV show called *The White Shadow*. He was playing a gang kid. A very mild version of what I ultimately cast him as. And Roddy McDowall was always a favourite of mine from the *Planet of the Apes* films. And then Michael J. Fox was on a TV series too, he had just started on *Family Ties*, so my film was his first movie.

DMB: *Class of 1984* is gleefully exploitative at times. When you were coming up with the ways that the gang members

64

were going to be killed, were you ever concerned about how far you were going to go?

ML: No, I wasn't concerned at all. In the '80s, there wasn't the feeling of self-censorship that there is today. I wasn't self-censoring myself; I just went as far out as I thought. The censors obviously had other ideas [*Laughs*]. There are things I don't think you could put in a film today. It's so politically correct. But I didn't have any of that pressure back then.

DMB: Do you have a favourite memory of the shoot?

ML: It was all fantastic. Every day of filming, I was just so happy. But there were weird things. When we shot the scene where Roddy McDowall's character finds his animals butchered by the gang, we went to an animal morgue. Those are all dead animals. I could barely walk on the set because the smell was so horrendous. It was unbelievable. They quickly nailed up all these dead animals and we shot the scene. I don't think we would be doing that in today's world, right?

DMB: What do you think audiences would take from the film now, compared to what they would have taken from it when it was released in the '80s?

ML: It was a shocking movie. Ronald Reagan mentioned it in a speech as President; 'Time Magazine' ran an editorial on the film. It was extremely controversial at the time, you know, it was even hard to get distributed, I had to go directly to the theatre chains to book it, because the studios were afraid it was too violent and too anti-establishment. From today's perspective, I don't know, people love the movie now as a cult movie from the era. Now events like Columbine or the Sandy Hook Elementary School shootings are way beyond this movie.

DMB: How did you get involved with *Firestarter* (1984)?

ML: I had never read a Stephen King book. I got a call from Dino De Laurentiis, and he said: "I just saw *Class of 1984*. Let's work together." He asked what my next project was. I was heading home from the Cannes Film Festival, and I remembered a story about Orson Welles. He was at this trade station, and he needed more money for *Macbeth* (1948). And he called the studio. And they asked, well, give us your next picture. So, he says "hold on." And he left the phone, and he went to one of those paperback spinners and he just grabbed a book and he said: "okay, my next movie is *The Lady from Shanghai*."
So, when De Laurentiis asked me for a project, I went to this book rack, and I spun it. And there was a book, 'Year of the Dragon' by Robert Daley. I picked this book and I said: "I want to make *Year of the Dragon*." He said: "great!" I had the script written with Daley, but then suddenly, Dino said: "I have this deal to make *Firestarter* so forget that movie. That's going to take too long. Let's do *Firestarter* right

now." So, I read my first Stephen King book!

DMB: Did you also read the previous script written when John Carpenter was signed up to direct *Firestarter*?

ML: I read that script and I went, yeah, they got rid of that project because it had nothing to do with the book at all. It was the complete opposite.

DMB: Can you talk about working with Tangerine Dream on the score?

ML: That was a done deal. Dino just wanted Tangerine Dream to score the movie. It was his idea. And I met with the band in LA to discuss the soundtrack. I showed Edgar Froese the film and the band wrote the score. I wasn't there when they composed the score in Berlin. They finished the music, and they sent back the tapes. I called him up, and I said: "Edgar, none of these tapes are labelled, where do we put them in the movie?" He says: "anywhere you want! It's music, it's not scored to specific scenes in the movie, it's just music for the movie." I go: "What? Put it wherever I want?!?" But it worked great. Only they could have thought of that. I never would have just said, give us music and we'll put it where we want.

DMB: At the time Drew Barrymore had just made *E.T. The Extra-Terrestrial*.
ML: Well, we read a lot of girls, a lot of little girls, but she was always our first choice. Heather O'Rourke from *Poltergeist* (1982) was our second choice but Drew Barrymore, she was so enthusiastic about the role, and she kept coming in for meetings and she'd say: "I just love this. I've got to do it." She was already very showbiz savvy,

even at the age of eight years old.

DMB: And then the rest of the cast, I mean, Martin Sheen, David Keith, Heather Locklear, George C. Scott. That's a dream cast right there.
ML: It was a fantastic cast. And we were only trying to get Oscar winners [*Laughs*]. I think there were five cast members that had been honoured with an Academy Award in *Firestarter*. George C. Scott, I was just in awe of him. Louise Fletcher won an Academy Award for *One Flew Over the Cuckoo's Nest* (1975), she was fantastic to work with. Art Carney, I was a fan of his in *The Honeymooners*. On set, he said: "I have a great idea. This farmer should wear a hearing aid." I go: "yeah, that's a cool idea." He says: "oh good, because I can't hear a thing without it." David Keith came off *An Officer and a Gentleman* (1982) and then Martin Sheen had already done *Apocalypse Now* (1979). It was amazing. Heather Locklear - we looked around for a lot of girls. She really had just done a milk commercial and *TJ Hooker* with William Shatner. And Dino, he had some deal with Jack Gillard, her agent. They were close. So, she got into the picture and she›s fantastic. She was so beautiful. It was unbelievable.

DMB: And then came *Commando* (1985). Working with Arnold Schwarzenegger must have been an experience.
ML: He is an amazing human being. That was the movie he made right after *The Terminator* (1984). Everyone acknowledges that I developed this persona for him. I

was thinking James Bond style quips. Arnold has the greatest sense of humour. He was always joking and cracking one-liners. I told the writer: "you've got to put these in the movie, and I'll come up with some myself, but we must use humour throughout this movie." And our producer Joel Silver agreed. He had just made *48 Hrs* (1982). And he said he was of the notion that that picture did well because of Eddie Murphy. And nobody wanted Eddie Murphy because he was a comic. But put him in an action movie and you get laughs as well. And that's why there's some funny lines in *Commando*. I remember going to the first screening when the film first opened, and I went with all the studio executives to Westwood to watch it with the real audience.

And before Arnold said "I lied" the whole audience shouted out the line. And I looked to Larry Gordon, the head of the studio, and I said: "how do they know that line?" He says: "It's in the trailer. That's why it's in the trailer." It was like watching *The Rocky Horror Picture Show* (1975) with explosions!

DMB: The action set pieces are explosive. Did you enjoy working on a bigger production?
ML: I loved it because I had access to all this equipment. It was mind-boggling. Like, the whole airplane sequence. We were able to shoot at LAX in those days with a fix, a fake giant tire that was on a flatbed truck and Arnie was hanging on. I always thought that Arnold, since he was Mr. Universe, he could do the things that were in the script for himself, right? There is a scene where he carries Sully, played by David Patrick Kelly, across the road and hangs him over a cliff. He's holding on to him by both of his feet, So, the night before the shoot, I called Arnold to check he is ready. I tell him that tomorrow, he's going to pick up Sully out of the car and hold him by his feet, walk across the road, and hang him over the cliff. He says: "Are you crazy?" I go: "well, no, that's in the script. I thought you

were Mr. Universe. David is a short light guy, so you'll be able to lift him. I looked it up. He could lift 500 pounds. It is nothing." But he said: "I can't carry a man and hold them like that and then do a scene. That's impossible." I thought oh, my God, what do we do? The scene is in the morning. So, I called the studio in a panic, and we got a crane. We hung the actor using a wire rig. Arnold is just pretending to hold him.

DMB: The film is very violent, especially the tool shed scene when Arnie throws a circular saw at one soldier's head and chops off another's arm...
ML: Arnold kept saying: "Mark, I want to cut one of these soldiers arms off with an axe. And then I want to pick up the severed limb and slap him in the face with his own hand." And I said: "that's ridiculous." We never did do it. But he really wanted to do that in the worst way.

DMB: Rae Dawn Chong was great in the film.
ML: Yeah, fantastic. And there again, we read every girl in Hollywood including Sharon Stone who ended up doing *Total Recall* (1990) with Arnold. Rae came in, just did a reading, and she was so funny. We were looking for humour again, and

that's how she got that part. She was very funny. She was perfect in that role.

DMB: Your last film of the decade was a change of pace. Can you talk about *Armed and Dangerous* (1986)?
ML: Well, they offered it to me, and I thought, okay, well, it's different, and it mixes humour and action. Comedy really wasn't my forte and it's probably too violent for a comedy because there's some typically Lester action scenes, but I just thought why not try it?

DMB: And you cast Meg Ryan and John Candy?
ML: It was one of Meg Ryan's first movies. She was brought in by the casting people. She had just been in *Top Gun* for Tony Scott. And John Candy, he's a wonderful person. He had some health issues at the time, but he was great to work with. And Eugene Levy whose doing great things now with *Schitt's Creek*. They were funny, funny guys.

DMB: At least with a comedy you would not have been censored.
ML: But we were! A really funny moment was censored. When John Candy and Eugene Levy visit a porno store and they held up a rubber dildo, there's a line: "Put that down. You don't know where it's been." That was cut out. Eugene is wearing leather chaps. It was very funny to me.

DMB: Is it right that Dan Aykroyd was going to be working on the film before Eugene Levy was given the role?
ML: That was Dan Aykroyd's role, and he dropped out at the last minute. Eugene Levy wasn't really known at the time. He had done *Splash* but he wasn't really a name like Dan Aykroyd was. And that kind of enticed me to the project, too. The chance to work with John Candy and Dan Aykroyd. And then two weeks before shooting he didn't want to do it. And then Levy stepped in.

DMB: And the film had another *Stripes* connection?
ML: Harold Ramis wrote the script. There was another guy that worked with him, and Harold would just walk around the room dictating the script because the first version wasn't very good.

DMB: How do you look back on the '80s?
ML: I've been very blessed and very lucky. I've directed 35 movies and produced another 50 movies in my career. The '80s were amazing years for me. I came into my own. People don't realise it had been a ten-year journey to get there. By the time I made *Class of 1984*, I already had ten years' experience making drive-in flicks like *Steel Arena* (1973) and *Truck Stop Women* (1974). So, I was just at the right prime to make those '80s films, and a couple became classics. You could be as creatively free as you wanted, which is why it was great to be a filmmaker in the '80s. That's how it was.

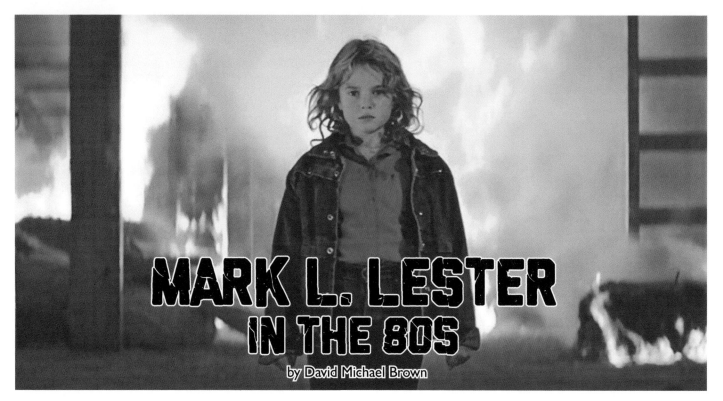

MARK L. LESTER IN THE 80S

by David Michael Brown

In the '80s, the British Board of Classification did not like Mark L. Lester. *Class of 1984* (1982) and *Commando* (1985) both fell victim to the censor's scissors in the wake of sensationalist "video nasty" headlines being splashed across the front covers of newspapers and the horrors of the Video Recordings Act 1984 being felt on the shelves of local video stores up and down the country. In a decade that also saw the director adapt Stephen King's *Firestarter* (1984) and helm comedy royalty in the laugh-filled actioner *Armed and Dangerous* (1986), two of his most enjoyable films proved impossible to see in uncut form for many years.

Lester - born in Cleveland, Ohio - made his debut with *Steel Arena* (1973) and followed it with a succession of drive-in classics, including *Truck Stop Women* (1974) starring 1970 Playboy Playmate of the Year Claudia Jennings, and *Bobbie Jo and the Outlaw* (1976) with Marjoe Gortner and Wonder Woman herself, Lynda Carter. In 1977, he directed the high-concept thriller *Stunts* for New Line Cinema which boasted the poster tagline: "Dying is one hell of a way to make a living." In 1979, while everyone was still strutting their stuff to the Bee Gees and John Travolta in *Saturday Night Fever* (1977), he jumped on the disco bandwagon to helm *Roller Boogie* (1979) starring Linda Blair, beating Olivia Newton-John's *Xanadu* (1980) to the roller disco by a year.

Class of 1984 (1982)

Having read a sensationalist review of *Class of 1984* in the British fantasy magazine 'Starburst', the film was on top of my 'to-watch' list. Unfortunately, this cautionary tale of high school violence was cut by four minutes and

fourteen seconds by the BBFC for its 1982 cinema release, and, despite never officially joining the horrific hallowed ranks of the Director of Public Prosecutions list of banned films, it was refused a video certificate four years later. When I eventually watched an imported VHS, it was still a version which had been cut by the MPAA. It was many years before I managed to witness Lester's original vision in its outrageous splendour.

Class of 1984 was Lester's brilliant fusion of preachy '50s juvenile delinquent flick, sleazy '80s gorefest and gritty '70s realism, inspired by a loud and brash US punk scene led by Black Flag, the Dead Kennedys and the Bad Brains. Deliberately provocative and gleefully controversial, it's no surprise Lester's lurid exploitation flick had censorship troubles wherever it was released. Or maybe nobody liked the fact that Lester almost killed off a young Michael J. Fox!

The opening card sets the scene: "Last year there were 280,000 incidents of violence by students against teachers and their classmates in American high schools. Unfortunately, this film is based on true events. Fortunately, very few schools are like Lincoln High… yet."

Class of 1984, co-written *by Fright Night* director Tom Holland, stars *Mandingo*'s Perry King as Andrew Norris, a big-hearted music teacher who takes a new position at an inner-city high school (Central Technical School in Toronto Canada masquerading as Abraham Lincoln High) with an idealistic vision that he can change these young kid's lives. How wrong he is. The school corridors are ruled by a vicious bunch of thuggish punks. Armed with cutthroat razors which they smuggle past the school metal detectors, they terrorise the kids who want to learn and the teachers whose unenviable job it is to teach them. Biology teacher Mr. Corrigan (Roddy McDowall) takes the new teacher under his wing and a gun to class as he tries to survive one school day at a time.

The gang make Norris' life a misery and what begins as harassment soon turns to murder as the gang rape his wife. The teacher's bloody retribution includes dispatching the thugs by such means as a circular saw and a blow torch. The rape scene caused particular consternation for the BBFC but, as Lester commented when promoting the newly uncut Blu-ray: "that scene is not played for gratuitous thrills. It shows rape for what it is, an ugly, nasty act. And it's necessary to show it because we understand what drives Perry King's character to commit such a brutal act of revenge against his tormentors."

The gang is led by well-coiffured Peter Stegman (Timothy Van Patten). Seemingly untouchable, a nihilistic rich kid who happens to be a piano virtuoso, he is also a twisted psychotic thug who hides behind his white privilege. He may look like a member of New Romantic popsters Spandau Ballet, but the vicious Hitler youth seethes with hatred for anyone who doesn't adhere to his fascist worldview. The rest of the gang includes Lisa Langlois as Patsy (Stegman's girlfriend and the gang's only female member), Stefan Arngrim as junkie Drugstore, Keith Knight as the thuggish Barnyard and Neil Clifford as the mohawked Fallon.

Of the gang, it was Arngrim whose life added authenticity to his role. The member of punk band The Wild Boys told Kier-la Janisse in the indispensable guide to punks in film 'Destroy All Movies': "I was living in London in 1976 and misspent a good portion of my waning youth on the King's Road at SEX, which was Viv Westwood and Malcolm McLaren's clothing store. I saw the Pistols, Clash, Slits and Siouxsie at Club 100, took many drugs and got beaten up a few times!" It was Arngrim who helped Lester cast the punks who frequented the clubs in the film, and he also talked Teenage Head into playing in the film. Langlois, also interviewed in the book, said of the cast: "Other than the

actors themselves, we didn't really hire any professionals; it was all real punk people. When we had those big dance scenes in clubs, those people didn't know how to do stunts so they would just do the real thing - slamming people - so the principal actors were getting hurt."

Watched now in all its uncut glory, Lester's exploitationer is a shocking revelation far beyond the sanitised version the censors saw fit to show us. As Roger Ebert said on its release in 1982: *"Class of 1984 is raw, offensive, vulgar and violent, but it contains the sparks of talent and wit, and it is directed by people who cared to make it special."*

Firestarter (1984)

Following in the footsteps of Brian De Palma's *Carrie* (1976), Stanley Kubrick's *The Shining* (1980), John Carpenter's *Christine* (1983), Lewis Teague's *Cujo* (1983) and David Cronenberg's *The Dead Zone* (1983), Lester helmed his own Stephen King adaptation in 1984.

With an ensemble that boasted David Keith, Drew Barrymore, Martin Sheen, Louise Fletcher, Heather Locklear and George C. Scott, a score by Krautrock maestros Tangerine Dream and adapted from a novel by one of the world's most successful novelists, there was a lot riding on the incendiary tale of telekinetic firestarting. Despite the talents involved, the film - handed to Lester by producer Dino De Laurentiis after John Carpenter dropped out - failed to excite the critics like previous King adaptations and it failed to ignite the box office.

It sticks to the events of King's book closely (after all, Dino de Laurentis paid $1million for the rights), and follows Andy McGee (Keith) and his future wife Vicky (Locklear), a young couple who participated in secret experiments during which they were subjected to mysterious medical tests. Years later, their young daughter Charlie (Barrymore) begins to exhibit pyromaniac tendencies with her mind. These volatile pyrokinetic powers makes the youngster a target for the mysterious agency known as 'The Shop' who want to weaponise her talents.

"Stephen King came down to the set," Lester explained. "He was there with De Laurentiis. Dino said we can't just have Drew Barrymore staring and then fires start. Something must happen, magical or supernatural. And King said: 'yeah, let's have her hair blown. Like blowing.' So, we had all these hair-blowing machines. Every time

Charlie McGee is a happy, healthy
eight-year-old little girl.
Normal in every way but one.

She has the power to set objects afire
with just one glance.

It's a power she does not want.
It's a power she cannot control.
And, each night, Charlie prays
to be just like every other child.

But there are those who will do
everything in their power
to find her, control her...
or destroy her.

Charlie McGee is Stephen King's

FIRESTARTER

Will she have the power...to survive?

DINO DE LAURENTIIS presents
"FIRESTARTER"
Starring DAVID KEITH · DREW BARRYMORE
FREDDIE JONES · HEATHER LOCKLEAR · MARTIN SHEEN
GEORGE C. SCOTT · ART CARNEY · LOUISE FLETCHER
Screenplay by STANLEY MANN Based on the Novel by STEPHEN KING Music by TANGERINE DREAM
Associate Producer MARTHA SCHUMACHER Produced by FRANK CAPRA Jr. Directed by MARK LESTER
A UNIVERSAL RELEASE

COMING SOON TO A THEATRE NEAR YOU.

she starts a fire, her hair blows. They even use that in the sequel. Later, King said 'what a dumb idea it was.' But it was his idea."

When guesting on *The Drew Barrymore Show* in 2021, King maintained the wind machines were a good idea, even though he had gone on record as not liking Lester's adaptation. "I thought that you were terrific in that part. That was very, very difficult and you were great. Every time you got ready to light a fire, your beautiful blonde hair would blow back - it was great," he told Drew on her show.

"I loved getting to play Charlie McGee more than words can ever express and when you're seven and you think you can blow people away with a fireball, it's really empowering," Barrymore added. The young actress was fresh off working with Steven Spielberg on *E.T: The Extra-Terrestrial* (1982) and was perfectly cast as the young girl who made sparks fly.

The pyrotechnics are impressive considering that this was pre-digital FX and that most of the fires are caused by a young girl whose safety had to be ensured on set. Barrymore was often replaced by a diminutive body double during night shoots when her face did not need to be seen. "That film is absolutely the most difficult film I worked on," Lester told 'Daily Dead'. "We took one whole week working nonstop to finish the farm attack sequence at the end. It was all pretty nightmarish. What you see in that last act are practical effects. The fireballs… that's not CGI. Back then, we actually created fireballs that could fly through the air! They were on a wire and could crash into buildings. We had people on fire that were on trampolines that had to flip through the air. It was very dangerous. All the effects were done right on the set - it was a pretty intense thing to do then."

Tangerine Dream, the German electronic pioneers, were coming off a dream run including Paul Brickman's *Risky Business* (1983), the low-fi sci-fi *Wavelength* (1983) and Michael Mann's *The Keep* (1983) when they were signed up by De Laurentiis to provide the film's melodic score. At the time, the band comprised of founder Edgar Froese, Christophe Franke and Johannes Schmoelling. Edgar Froese spoke about their *Firestarter* score to 'Electronic Soundmaker & Computer Music' magazine: "The best way of doing soundtracks was on *Firestarter* where we had total freedom. Dino de Laurentiis flew in from Italy to watch some of it being done, then we went to LA to discuss the music with the director and we discussed everything as we went along. We did new mixes for the album; we produced the record, and it more or less gave it a unity which mirrored the way it was used in the film."

Watched now, *Firestarter* might lack *Cujo*'s bite or *Christine*'s studied '50s cool, but it remains a hugely enjoyable sci-fi-tinged scorcher. And despite not being top-tier King, the film, thanks to its starry cast and iconic soundtrack, remains one of Mark L. Lester's most beloved. No wonder the King adaptation was a major influence on the Duffer Brothers when creating the character of Eleven (Millie Bobby Brown) in the smash Netflix fantasy show *Stranger Things*.

Commando (1985)

The Cannon Royal cinema on Charing Cross Road, nestled in the shadow of the Odeon Leicester Square,

Somewhere, somehow, someone's going to pay.

SCHWARZENEGGER COMMANDO

TWENTIETH CENTURY FOX PRESENTS A SILVER PICTURES PRODUCTION ARNOLD SCHWARZENEGGER "COMMANDO" RAE DAWN CHONG MUSIC BY JAMES HORNER ASSOCIATE PRODUCERS JOSEPH LOEB III & MATTHEW WEISMAN SCREENPLAY BY STEVEN E. DE SOUZA STORY BY JOSEPH LOEB III & MATTHEW WEISMAN AND STEVEN E. DE SOUZA PRODUCED BY JOEL SILVER DIRECTED BY MARK L. LESTER

was a haven for the trashier side of cinema. From George A. Romero's *Day of the Dead* (1985) and Paul Verhoeven's *Flesh + Blood* (1985) to the Rutger Hauer thriller *The Hitcher* (1986) and Stuart Gordon's gore-fest *Re-animator* (1985), I watched them all there, including *Commando*.

The thrill of watching an extremely violent actioner starring Arnold Schwarzenegger on the big screen was tempered by the realisation that the graphic scenes of dismemberment promised in the hallowed pages of US periodicals like 'Fangoria' or 'Cinefantastique' had been brutally hacked by the BBFC. A feeling all-too-familiar to UK cinemagoers in the '80s.

Arnie's star was well and truly on the ascendant by the time he played John Matrix, a retired Special Forces colonel who is forced back into action when his daughter (a young Alyssa Milano) is kidnapped by mercenaries including Bennett (Vernon Wells), an ex-member of Matrix's team discharged for excessive violence.

With Rae Dawn Chong by his side as an air hostess he commandeers to help him, the heavily armed one-man wrecking machine wisecracks his way through explosive set-piece after explosive set-piece. The bad guys include Dan Hedaya, Bill Duke, and *The Warriors* star David Patrick Kelly who gives Matrix the run around before being dropped off a cliff.

It's the tool shed scene that is the most revelatory when watched uncut. The original UK cinema and video versions were censored by around 20 seconds, and removed the shots where Matrix cuts off the soldier's arm with the machete. Bennett's death was also trimmed to remove a shot of the pipe in his chest. Now watched in all its gory glory, soldiers are sliced with circular saw blades, an axe is wielded and the infamous arm is lopped off and thrown to the ground.

The final moment could have been even more gratuitous as Schwarzenegger described during a Reddit chat. "I wanted to cut off a guy's arm and kill him with it. This wasn't in the script. He would throw a knife at me and

73

after he missed, while his arm was still extended, I chop it off at the shoulder with a machete and beat him to death with it. Needless to say, I was asked by the head of the studio Larry Gordon to come to his office. And he said: 'what the fuck is the matter with you? Do you want to make money with this movie or an X-rated movie?' I said: 'you're right.' And he said: 'get the fuck out of my office.'"

It wasn't only the violence that was cut. An inter-racial sex scene between Arnie and Chong had worried the film studio. Lester explained: "The interesting thing is there was a love scene in the script. Matrix and Cindy make love on the way to the island in the plane. But since it was a black woman, in that era the studio was like: 'they'll never play the film in the south and the drive-ins in the south, we can't have black and white love scenes.' In terms of plot, it was OK because why is he stopping to make love while he's looking for his kidnapped daughter? So, we just intimated that they would have a relationship later. But that was cut from the script."

In *The Terminator* Schwarzenegger promised: "I'll be back" and *Commando* ensured he would. The rip-roaring actioner moves at breakneck speed and takes no prisoners. Arnie's tried and tested quipping persona ("Let off some steam, Bennett") works wonders and signposted the glory days ahead for the Teutonic titan.

Armed and Dangerous (1986)

After the huge success of *Commando*, Lester could have picked to do any movie. But the film he chose to direct was the little seen *Armed and Dangerous*. Critically reviled, this action-comedy failed to set the box office alight. Lester has admitted that the mixture of laughs, thrills and spills didn't quite gel. As he reflected in 2014: "The movie came out okay, but I wasn't used to working with comedians. I was trying to tell the story and put in some good action scenes, but they didn't care about any of that. They just wanted to be funny."

Looking back, the cast is top-heavy with comedic talent, but Lester cast them on their way up. John Candy had starred in *Stripes* (1981), *National Lampoon's Vacation* (1983), *Splash* (1984) and *Brewster's Millions* (1985) but *Armed & Dangerous* was only his second lead role in a Hollywood film after *Summer Rental* (1985), directed by Carl Reiner.

Meg Ryan had shone in a couple of scenes in Tony Scott's *Top Gun* after brief appearances in *Rich and Famous* (1981) and *Amityville 3-D* (1983), but the rom-com glory days were a way off. Eugene Levy had also appeared in *Vacation* and *Splash*, as well as *The Last Polka* (1985) which he wrote with his co-star John Candy.

Candy stars as Frank Dooley, a police officer who has been wrongly dismissed from his job after being framed for stealing a television set by two corrupt detectives.

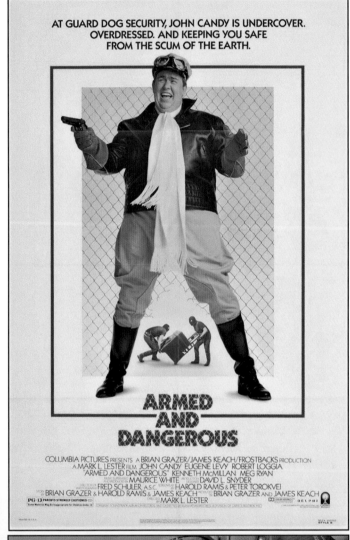

Finding employment as a security guard, he forms an uneasy friendship with Norman Kane (Eugene Levy), an inept lawyer. Unfortunately, the company that employs Frank and Norman is involved in some shady dealings, and it's up to the bumbling guards to foil the plans of the corrupt leaders, most notably tough mobster Michael Carlino (Robert Loggia), who isn't happy to have his profitable scheme threatened.

The project was initially developed by Harold Ramis as a vehicle for *Saturday Night Live* alumni Dan Aykroyd and John Belushi. In a coincidence, would-be *Firestarter* director John Carpenter was initially attached to direct marking the second time that Lester had taken over one of Carpenter's projects. Carpenter stated that he dropped out of the film after Aykroyd stipulated that he would not appear unless the script was changed to culminate with a car chase! Ramis was not happy with the final results and tried to get his name removed from the film, only succeeding in getting his executive producer credit removed.

The film is very much of its time. Some films from the '80s still shine but, despite the talent involved, *Armed & Dangerous* is a confused mix of genres. It's not that it isn't funny - the scene, for example, where Candy and Levy in disguise cruise a sex shop is dated but still raises laughs. Referring to the scene where Levy ends up looking uncomfortable in leather, Candy told the 'Los Angeles Times': "Mark [Lester] and I just broke up laughing when we saw Gene, but he said there was no way he was going to wear those pants. We just kept laughing and laughing, so Gene finally grumbled: 'OK. I'll do the leather, but *not* the cut-outs!'"

After experiencing the failure of *Armed and Dangerous*, Lester started the '90s as he'd begun the '80s, spilling blood in the schoolyard (this time in the future). *Class of 1999* (1990) took the gang warfare of *Class of 1984* and added robots and Stacy Keach for a story in which three ex-military robots are reprogrammed as teachers and secretly planted in a school to handle the gang problem. Alice Cooper may have claimed "I am the future" on the soundtrack to *Class of 1984*, but Mark L. Lester had other ideas!

MIDNIGHT RUN

by Peter Sawford

Throughout his career, Robert De Niro has tried his hand at most genres and, in recent years, has shown a particular affinity for comedy. Back in 1988, he was best known for tough and gritty roles in serious fare like *Mean Streets* (1973), *The Godfather II* (1974), *Taxi Driver* (1976), *Raging Bull* (1980) and *The Untouchables* (1987).

Midnight Run changed all that.

Directed by Martin Brest, working from an excellent script by George Gallo, *Midnight Run* casts De Niro as Jack Walsh, an ex-Chicago cop who now tracks down wanted criminals and bail skippers in Los Angeles. When he was in in Chicago, working undercover to bring down a drug dealer, he had narcotics planted in his house by corrupt fellow officers, forcing him to resign rather than go to prison. His wife left him and married one of his corrupt colleagues, taking their daughter with her. Justifiably upset, Jack moved to L.A. and became possibly the angriest bounty hunter in history.

De Niro clearly has a ball playing Jack, spitting venomous insults one minute, turning the air blue the next. He shows total irreverence to wannabe superiors, but occasionally exhibits a quieter, softer nature. De Niro draws upon years of experience, channelling dozens of previous roles, to make Jack a thoroughly rounded character with enough rough edges to be believable and interesting.

Jack is essentially a good person, but he has little-to-no patience and his temper seems permanently on a short fuse. He's generally law-abiding, though he has no issue bending the rules when necessary or breaking them completely if needs must. All Jack wants is to earn enough money to buy a little coffee shop, settle down and get out of the bounty hunting game for good.

This dream seems a step closer when bail bondsman Eddie Moscone (Joe Pantoliano) offers him an easy job - a so-called 'midnight run' - to bring in an accountant who embezzled $15 million from the Mob, then skipped bail on the $450,000 Moscone posted to keep him out of jail until his trial date. Moscone, understandably, would like his money back.

It looks like a simple enough task, and Jack makes light work of tracking down the accountant - Jonathan 'The Duke' Mardukas (superbly played by Charles Grodin) - who is hiding out in New York. On the journey back to Los Angeles, though, Mardukas proves to be the fugitive from hell. He claims to have given all the money he embezzled to charity, but the Mob noticed it was missing and now they want revenge. He has no intention of going along with Jack, knowing his days will be numbered if he ends up in custody - Mob boss Jimmy Serrano (Dennis Farina) will find a way to get him no matter where he's put or what the police do to protect him. Mardukas does everything in his power to make the journey from New York to Los Angeles as difficult and uncomfortable as possible, hoping to escape somewhere along the way.

Grodin turns in a career-best performance, effortlessly stealing the film from under De Niro's nose with such style and humour that I doubt De Niro minded one jot. Whether feigning a panic attack to get off a plane, endlessly trying to give Jack the slip, simply winding Jack up or, occasionally, going along with Jack's plans, Grodin's Mardukas is central to every scene he's in. We find ourselves pitying Jack for having to put up with this nit-picking neurotic who has enough quirks and idiosyncrasies to drive any sane person mad. But such is the strength of Grodin's performance that we also have sympathy for Mardukas, an amiable sort who has ended up tangled in a web of his own making even though he didn't know he was making it at the time.

Every now and again, Mardukas takes the lead to help them out a jam. In one memorable scene, he tells everyone in a bar that he and Jack are FBI agents on the trail of a counterfeiter who's been dropping fake $20 bills across the state. Pretending to check the $20s in the till, they steal as many as they can thanks to a 'litmus configuration' test which tells them which notes are good and which are bad. Grodin's interaction with the dark-haired bar owner - the 'Red' from Red's Bar - is inspired, as is his totally unscripted conversation with the extra playing the barfly who, to his credit, plays along superbly.

Thrown into the melting pot to make Jack's life that little bit more miserable is FBI Special Agent Alonzo Mosely (Yaphet Kotto), who's determined to bring in Mardukas to get him to testify against Serrano. Mosely is always one step behind, always a few minutes too late, and just a bit slow at noticing when his sunglasses or his FBI identification have been stolen! Kotto was best known for the dual role of Dr. Kananga/Mr. Big in *Live and Let Die* (1973) and the doomed Parker in *Alien* (1979). He'd just finished filming *The Running Man* (1987) with Arnold Schwarzenegger when the cameras started rolling on *Midnight Run*. Like De Niro, Kotto wasn't known for his comedic abilities but proves himself adept at the genre, despite being ill for most of the shoot. Kotto didn't have happy memories of *Midnight Run* or Martin Brest, but none of that comes through in his performance. His real-life irritation might even have helped with his irritable responses during his verbal sparring with Jack. His annoyance when everyone thinks all FBI agents are called Alonzo Mosely due to the number of times his stolen ID is used is priceless.

With Mardukas spoiling Jack's nice simple plan to get them back to the West coast, Moscone starts to believe Jack is making a mess of things and thinks he'll never see his $450,000 again. He secretly hires Marvin Dorfler (John Ashton), another bounty hunter, to sort things out. Marvin comes across like a slightly dim-witted younger brother to Sgt. Taggart, Ashton's character in the first two *Beverly Hills Cop* films. While Taggart had the common sense to keep his mouth shut, Marvin hasn't got that 'switch'

and endlessly talks himself into more trouble than he can handle. Even when he thinks he's triumphed by putting himself in a position to play the Mob off against everyone else, he fouls up by showing his hand too early, dropping himself in the deep end and taking another bruising for his trouble. We suspect he carries his scars like some sort of badge of honour. Ashton gives Marvin a wonderfully world-weary attitude. He acts like everyone else is an idiot, taking great pleasure in pointing out their shortcomings - he most certainly doesn't suffer fools gladly. Ashton has enjoyed a long and successful career, but I don't think he's ever been better than he is here.

Everything builds to a relatively happy ending (though Jimmy Serrano and Eddie Moscone might disagree) and Jack and Mardukas finally part ways. Just for a moment, there's a fear the story might lose its courage and have them wander off as newfound best friends to enjoy more adventures, but thankfully Brest has the good sense to

see their relationship through to its logical, if slightly bittersweet, conclusion.

There are a number of wonderful bit-parts in the film. At one point, Jack is forced to visit his ex-wife's house to borrow money and a car. For the first time in years, he sees his daughter Denise (Danielle DuClos). Uneasy at having not seen him for so long, young DuClos plays the scene superbly, exchanging awkward glances and clumsy hugs with a father she's never had the chance to get to know or love. Despite what her mother may have told her, she stills see the good in him and still loves him. Her offer to help by handing over all her babysitting money is as touching as De Niro's refusal to take it. He may be close to rock bottom, but even he is not low enough to accept his daughter's hard-earned money.

A less cute couple are Serrano's henchmen, Tony and Joey (Richard Foronjy and Robert Miranda) or "Moron #1 and Moron #2" and Serrano justifiably calls them. If a situation can be fouled up, Tony and (especially) Joey can be counted on to foul it up. They're like a couple of kids who, after being given free rein in a sweet shop, hyperactively rush into situations without pause for thought. They are so unreliable and bad at their jobs that you're left wondering how they've made it so far up the Mafia step ladder, but at the same time you never really want any harm to come to them.

Pantoliano is brilliant as the frantic bail bondsmen Eddie Moscone, a man for whom yelling is the standard form of communication and who always appears to be one explosive outburst away from a seizure. The only thing more impressive than his ability to erupt at a moment's notice is the outlandishness of his socks, in which he hides his reserve of spare cash.

Whenever information about Jack and The Duke's whereabouts comes in, Moscone's pal Jerry (Jack Kehoe), who mans the phones at the bail bonds office, finds some excuse - coffee, donuts or simply the need for some fresh air - to contact Serrano and pass it on. Playing both sides against the other is dangerous, but Jerry only has eyes for the pot of gold at the end of the rainbow and is prepared to do whatever it takes to get his share of it.

Director Brest's previous hit had been

Beverly Hills Cop (1984) for which he earned a Golden Globe nomination and which set him up perfectly for helming *Midnight Run*. Brest keeps the film moving at a cracking pace and never lets it slip, giving equal time to each character and making sure all their back-stories and traits shine through.

Made on a budget of $35 million, *Midnight Run* took over $85 million at the box office and earned its director a second Golden Globe nomination in the Best Director of a Musical or Comedy category. He lost out to Mike Nichols for *Working Girl*, a decision I'm still trying to work out.

The film was a critical and commercial success, and over the years its reputation has grown further still. It's now considered a classic of the buddy movie genre. In 2021, Universal Pictures announced plans for a sequel which, if I'm being honest, I hope never happens.

There were three made-for-television sequels - *Another Midnight Run*, *Midnight Runaround* and *Midnight Run for Your Life* (all 1994) - which disappeared almost as quickly as they appeared. Lots of films have great scripts, an excellent cast and fine direction, but not all become classics - sometimes a film just clicks for no discernible reason. *Midnight Run* has that extra something which elevates it above the norm. It's not easy to catch lightning in a bottle once, almost impossible to do so twice.

As we near the 35th anniversary of the film's release, it's sad to reflect that Charles Grodin, Yaphet Kotto and Dennis Farina are no longer with us. Although they left us with many great performances and films, I'll always remember them for *Midnight Run*. Some films can play tricks on you, and when you rewatch them years later they don't live up to your memories. They're not as funny, exciting or thrilling as you remember from your first viewing. *Midnight Run* is different - it exceeds expectations and improves every time you revisit it. It simply doesn't date, looking as inventive and fresh and funny as the day it was released. You certainly don't need a litmus configuration test to tell you that!

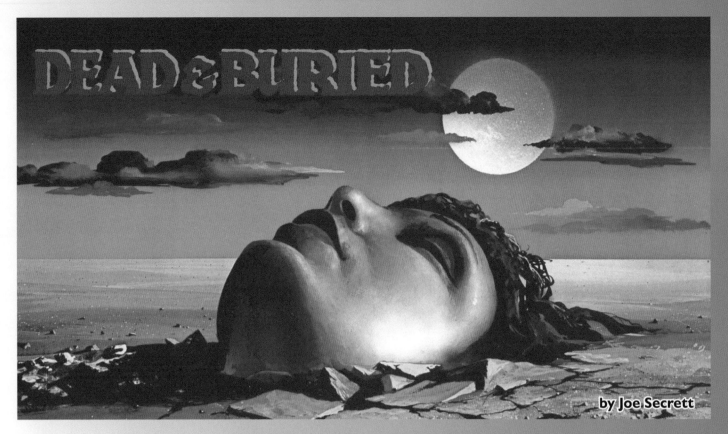

DEAD&BURIED

by Joe Secrett

"Welcme to Potter's Bluff" - one the nicest yet scariest lines from the 1981 horror film *Dead & Buried*.

A photographer arrives in the sleepy coastal town of Potter's Bluff with the intention of capturing some seaside snaps. Unexpectedly, a young woman shows up and offers to model for him. Within moments, she bares all for the camera and he thinks he's about to get a little extra "commission" for his photographic skills. Just as he's about to indulge himself with the flirtatious woman, a group of locals turn up and attack him, stringing him up in a fishing net before swiftly immolating him. All the while, the attackers take pictures and film him while he burns. What's even more horrific, the victim is later seen going about his day in the very town where he was slain, alive

and well and acting as if nothing happened.

It seems Potter's Bluff has become a hotspot for a series of brutal murders. Sheriff Dan Gillis (James Farentino) is desperate to find the culprit. Little does he know he's about to uncover a whole lot more than he reckoned on. Working with the eccentric town mortician Dobbs (Jack Albertson), Gillis learns of ancient tales of immortality and the extent to which people will go to achieve it.

Combining gruesome, sudden attacks with a sense of rising tension and mystery, *Dead & Buried* didn't really find an appreciative audience upon release in 1981. Since then, it has slowly built a reputation as a first-rate - if still underseen - horror classic, which takes an old, overused horror cliché (in this case, the rise of the undead) and

takes it back to its roots, incorporating strong hints of voodoo and witchcraft. With its strange premise and palpable atmosphere, *Dead & Buried* is now often cited as a true sleeper of the '80s. It is bolstered by a great cast playing the unsettling town's population, among them the soon-to-be-Freddie-Kreuger Robert Englund, Melody Anderson from the previous year's *Flash Gordon*, and future Golden Globe nominee Lisa Blount.

Farentino was mainly a TV stalwart, but he had occasional roles in theatrical features - *Dead & Buried* and *The Final Countdown* (1980) are probably his

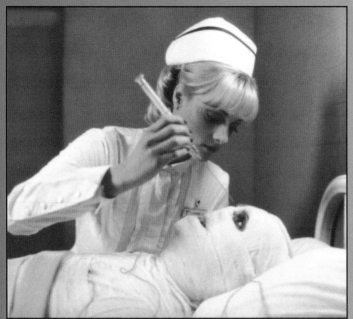

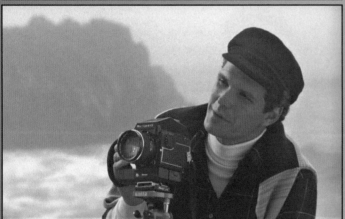

most well-known films. He also appeared in some of the most successful TV series of the day, such as *Dynasty*, *Ironside* and the mini-series *Jesus of Nazareth*. He brings a vulnerability to the character of Gillis as he tackles the investigation, trying to solve the daily murders but finding little to no help. His wife (Anderson) demonstrates increasingly bizarre behaviour, and her fascination with witchcraft only serves to deviate him as he struggles to put the pieces together. It's a shame Farentino did so few thrillers, as he's really good in this one - indeed, I'd go so far as to call it his career-best work.

The town mortician Dobbs offers a great last live-action role to the wonderful Jack Albertson. He was known and beloved by audiences for playing Grandpa Joe in *Willy Wonka and the Chocolate Factory* (1971) and Ed Brown (the Man) in the hit American TV show *Chico and the Man* (1974-78). Having him in such a dark and violent picture as this is a jarring shift in expectations but it works exceptionally well. He brings a cosy charm and charismatic presence to the role, at odds with the grisly underlying themes. Arriving at crime scenes with big band music playing on his car radio, Dobbs seems like someone who's not quite on the ball, as shown by his dark humour and over-commitment to his craft. He and Gillis frequently clash about their theories regarding the murders, and the script provides them with fleshed-out and informative conversations which keep the mystery afloat.

The special effects by Stan Winston are truly remarkable. Highlights include graphic throat slashings, a poor victim's head being crushed by a large rock, and a gruesome demise

wherein chemical tubes are shoved inside someone's nose. The best-known sequence has an unfortunate victim on the receiving end of a needle in the eye and Winston went all-out to create this effect, constructing a life-sized mechanical dummy for that one specific scene. Through his long and varied career, Winston has created effects which hold up extremely well, and his work on *Dead & Buried* stands out as some of the most accomplished and realistic visions of violence he ever put on screen. One death scene involving a dissolving head was not attributed to Winston. Another team was brought in to create it and, while still quite grisly, it's not quite up to the standard of the earlier kills.

The director Gary Sherman was no stranger to the horror genre, having been responsible for the UK/US production *Death Line* (1972) which remains a stone-cold classic to this day. He was also at the helm for the 1982 police thriller *Vice Squad* starring Wings Hauser and the third and final *Poltergeist* film in 1988. Much like *Dead & Buried*, these other films have garnered large followings long after their initial theatrical run.

A gloomy, foggy atmosphere pervades throughout *Dead & Buried*, even during the daytime scenes. It really adds to the uneasy sense of fear which looms over the town. Sherman wanted to keep the smattering of crimson to a minimum for much of the duration, so that when the bloody and gory stuff does occur it is more intense and shocking for the audience. He even changed car brake-lights to purple to avoid showing too much red away from the shock moments. Sherman originally toyed with the idea of presenting the film as a black comedy, but in the end the horror aspects prevailed. It would have been interesting to see how a blackly comic approach affected the story, but the lean and scary horror product we got instead is well worth the payoff.

With a twist ending which wouldn't seem out of place in an episode of *Tales of the Unexpected* or *The Twilight Zone*, *Dead & Buried* is a criminally unheralded horror gem. With terrific performances, creepily atmospheric locales and great spin on a classic horror trope, it deserves wider recognition and love.

"Welcome to Potter's Bluff." If you haven't seen it, what are you waiting for? Accept this warm and bloody invitation and give *Dead & Buried* a spin.

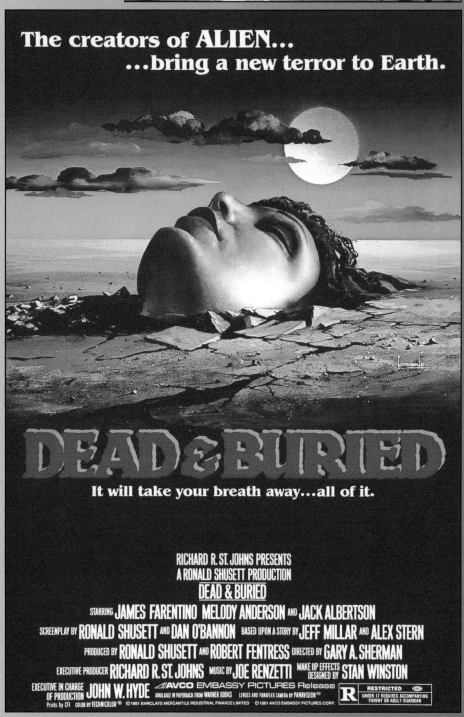

The creators of ALIEN...
...bring a new terror to Earth.

DEAD & BURIED

It will take your breath away...all of it.

RICHARD R. ST. JOHNS PRESENTS
A RONALD SHUSETT PRODUCTION
DEAD & BURIED
STARRING JAMES FARENTINO MELODY ANDERSON AND JACK ALBERTSON
SCREENPLAY BY RONALD SHUSETT AND DAN O'BANNON BASED UPON A STORY BY JEFF MILLAR AND ALEX STERN
PRODUCED BY RONALD SHUSETT AND ROBERT FENTRESS DIRECTED BY GARY A. SHERMAN
EXECUTIVE PRODUCER RICHARD R. ST. JOHNS MUSIC BY JOE RENZETTI MAKE UP EFFECTS DESIGNED BY STAN WINSTON
EXECUTIVE IN CHARGE OF PRODUCTION JOHN W. HYDE AVCO EMBASSY PICTURES Release
AVAILABLE IN PAPERBACK FROM WARNER BOOKS LENSES AND PANAFLEX CAMERA BY PANAVISION
Prints by CFI COLOR BY TECHNICOLOR © 1981 BARCLAYS MERCANTILE INDUSTRIAL FINANCE LIMITED © 1981 AVCO EMBASSY PICTURES CORP.
RESTRICTED
UNDER 17 REQUIRES ACCOMPANYING PARENT OR ADULT GUARDIAN

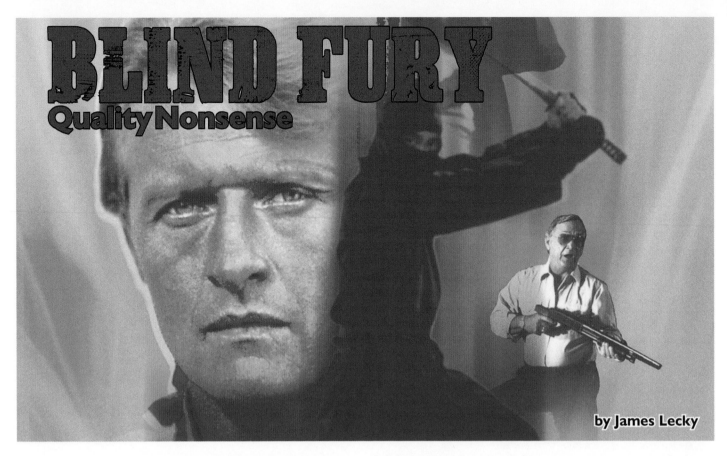

by James Lecky

Since at least the introduction of sound, every cinematic decade has been marked by its own distinctive genre.

The '30s saw the emergence of gangster films and musicals as popular forms. The '40s gave birth to film noir, the '50s to a series of science fiction films which mined the Red Scare and the threat of the Other. The '60s lay in the shadow of James Bond and his various imitators, while the '70s were dominated by the thriller in its many forms, often anti-establishment in outlook, with renegade cops and vigilantes to the fore (to the extent where even an ageing John Wayne was persuaded to hop on the *Dirty Harry* bandwagon with *McQ* [1974] and the London-set *Brannigan* [1975]).

The '80s saw the rise and dominance of the action film - and action hero - in movies that were loud, bright, improbable and violent. The protagonists - almost exclusively male - were practically superheroes: quick-witted, able to both dish it out and take it on the chin, absorbing and shrugging off the kind of damage that would send ordinary mortals into intensive care. Sub-plots were kept to a minimum (or preferably eliminated altogether), allowing for a lean narrative.

The action hero, and in particular the '80s action hero, is defined by *deeds* not *words*.

The apotheosis of the action film was probably *Commando* (1985), which saw Arnold Schwarzenegger's John Matrix rack up a three-digit, largely bloodless kill count while firing his M-60 one-handed from the hip.

The mores of the action film were quickly lampooned -

Schwarzenegger sent up his own screen persona in *Last Action Hero* (1993) while Charlie Sheen's Ramboesque rampage in *Hot Shots: Part Deux* (1993) managed a bodycount of nearly three hundred to great comic effect.

Its remit was broad (war, fantasy science fiction, crime, martial arts), its appeal international, and the stars drawn into its orbit included Schwarzenegger, Sylvester Stallone, Bruce Willis, Cynthia Rothrock, Chuck Norris, Dolph Lundgren, Jean-Claude Van Damme, Jackie Chan and Chow Yun-Fat, amongst others. Budgets ranged from the extravagant (over $60 million for *Rambo III* [1988]) right down to the realms of Poverty Row (half a million dollars for Jean-Claude Van Damme's breakthrough film *Cyborg* [1989]).

At its best, the '80s action film is pure and unapologetic mayhem - great fun when done right.

And Phillip Noyce's *Blind Fury* (1989) is done right.

Permanently blinded in a Vietcong attack, GI Nick Parker (Rutger Hauer) is nursed back to health by friendly villagers who teach him to compensate by fine-tuning his other senses and in addition (handily for the plot) to wield a sword with deadly accuracy. Years later, back in the USA, he seeks out an old army buddy Frank Devereaux (Terry O'Quinn) only to discover that he is missing and, unbeknownst to him, in thrall to the Reno Mob who want him to produce designer drugs. When Frank refuses to co-operate, Mob boss MacCready (Noble Willingham) sends his henchman Slag (Randall 'Tex' Cobb) to kidnap Frank's son Billy (Brandon Call) in order to use him for

leverage. The attempt is foiled by the sword-swinging Nick but Billy's mother, Frank's ex-wife Lynne (Meg Foster), is killed. With her dying breath she entrusts her son to Nick, asking him to reunite the boy with his father. But the Mob still wants Billy. And so the scene is set.

The action film can be a broad church and, in some ways, it is more a matter of style than content that defines it. The clue, of course, is in the nomenclature. These are not introspective works: incident piles upon incident, car chases, gunfights, fistfights and explosions abound, and one-man armies often take on overwhelming odds.

At its heart, *Blind Fury* is both a road movie and a buddy film in the classic mode whereby two mismatched characters are brought together through circumstance. Initially hostile, they come to accept, respect and, yes, even love one another (in the most macho way possible, of course). It is also much more light-hearted than most of its contemporaries, who's humour tends to consist of Bondesque quips (or possibly the "Ice to see you" style one-liners of Rainier Wolfcastle's McBain) to offset their violence.

Hauer is beautifully cast as Nick, a little smile never too far away and his actions sometimes bordering on the slapstick (particularly in an early scene where he deals with a group of thugs in a diner with a "whoops, sorry, did I just hit you with my cane?" routine that establishes the character's bona fides).

In fact, the whole film is imbued with a certain slapstick sensibility. Its villains are big and brash – as personified by Randall 'Tex' Cobb and his two redneck sidekicks Lyle and Tector Pike (Nick Cassavetes and Rick Overton), characters named after three members of Peckinpah's *The Wild Bunch* (1969). Cobb in particular chews the scenery almost as much as he chews on his cigar and has the odd great line ("Not bad for a blind man. But that butterknife ain't gonna stop no bullet.") which elevates him above the more run-of-the-mill bad guy. A former professional boxer (amongst other things), Cobb had already played a similar character (to more comic effect) in the Coen Brothers' *Raising Arizona* (1987) and would continue to mine his snarling bad guy persona throughout his career.

Pursued by Slag and his motley crew from Miami to Reno, Nick and Billy form an initially grudging bond, but not before a few well-shot and timed set pieces, in particular a cornfield chase which sees Nick rescue Billy from Slag once again, using his heightened senses to locate his enemies (never munch on a bag of popcorn around Nick Parker, as the aptly named Popcorn [Weasel Forshaw] learns a little too late.) Slag, however, survives this encounter thanks to the bulletproof (and presumably sword-proof) armour he conveniently wears.

Driven to distraction and under threat of being shut down by bigger and more unpleasant mobsters, MacCready demands that his underling Ed Cobb (Charles Cooper) does something about the situation - "If you can't handle it, get me somebody who can! Get me Bruce Lee! "Bruce Lee is dead." "Then get his brother!"

When Nick and Billy reach Reno they contact Frank's girlfriend Annie Winchester (Lisa Blount) only to be ambushed by the Pike Brothers. Nick is knocked unconscious, and he, Billy and Annie are taken to MacCready, but Nick arranges a daring escape during which Lyle and Tector are comically subdued and Nick retrieves his lost sword-cane.

As the Pike Brothers, Cassavettes and Overton are a fun if dim-witted double act (when they hijack an elderly woman's car only to have her fire an enormous pistol after them Tector remarks: "That's why I voted for gun control.")

The ensuing car chase sees Nick forced to drive (Annie's glasses have been broken and, like Velma Dinkley, she cannot see without her glasses) with Billy shouting directions and Lyle and Tector in hot pursuit ending up in a budget-friendly Dukes of Hazzard-style crash. (On a side note, two other redneck brothers named Lyle and Tector Gorch, in a more overt *Wild Bunch* homage, would turn up in seasons two and three of *Buffy the Vampire Slayer*).

With Billy and Annie safe for the moment, Nick sets out to rescue Frank.

After instigating a near-riot in the Cobb-MacCready Casino (into which Lyle and Tector, none the worse for their crash, happily wade) he confronts the bushy-browed Cobb (giving him an eyebrow trim during the process) and is able to reach Frank at last and, after destroying the illegal drug lab, the two escape.

But MacCready, it would appear, has a long reach and has already taken Billy and Annie and demands his drug shipment as payment for their safety. So Nick and Frank

gird their loins and armed with a sword and some "bathtub napalm" go to the rescue at MacCready's ski lodge high in the mountains.

Prefaced by some spectacular mountain scenery, the final act of *Blind Fury* is one of its many strengths.

Cleverly, Noyce and his screenwriter Charles Robert Carner strip away much of the humour that had hitherto marked the film. The violence may have been frequent but it was practically bloodless.

Here, abandoned by Frank (as once before in Vietnam), wounded by his enemies, outnumbered, outgunned and hunted through dismal corridors and dim rooms, Nick's superhero facade is stripped away, his heightened senses as much a curse as a blessing when he stumbles into a drum kit and active PA system in MacCready's private theatre.

But when the power is cut (by the returning Frank, of course) and the room plunged into blackness he is, metaphorically, reborn.

And here, too the nature of the film's violence changes. Prior to this, the power of Nick's sword had mostly been shown in the abstract - when a corrupt cop is slashed, the shelves behind him fall as well, a single blow is enough to take another corrupt cop's hand off (in a nod to both Kurosawa and George Lucas), bring down a shack or slice through a metal doorknob - but here it is given a certain level of savagery, culminating in the evisceration of Ed Cobb.

The smiling man with the cane has been replaced by an implacable killer stalking the darkness - "I can't see a thing." "That's where I live."

Had the film explored this version of Nick, it would have been a very different journey.

When Nick and Frank finally confront MacCready, he has another surprise waiting for them: Bruce Lee's brother, or rather a mysterious Japanese swordsman (Sho Kosugi).

The swordfight between Hauer and Kosugi is impeccably done and if the odd comical expression from Hauer might rob it of a little impact it is nevertheless impressive for all that.

In the end, of course, everything works out for the best: Nick defeats The Assassin, kills Slag with Billy's help, Frank

and his son (and Annie) are reunited and a tearful Nick walks off into the sunset, but retains a keepsake - a toy dinosaur that belonged to Billy, thrown away in a fit of pique.

It's a "Shane, Shane, come back Shane" moment utterly in keeping with the film. But then again, as already noted with Lyle and Tector, *Blind Fury* is happy to wear its influences on its sleeve.

The initial spark came from the hugely successful Japanese film series about Zatoichi, a blind swordsman in feudal Japan. Producer Tim Matheson - who had made his initial impact as an actor, appearing in *National Lampoon's Animal House* (1978) and alongside Kurt Russell in the western TV series *The Quest* (1976) - had been a fan of the series and wanted to do an American version. *Blind Fury* is very loosely based on *Zatoichi Challenged* (1967), but the concept of the blind hero had been used before (*Blindman* [1971], a spaghetti western starring Tony Anthony and directed by Ferdinano Baldi), would be used again (*Blind Justice* [1994], an outstanding made-for-TV western starring Armand Assante and directed by Richard Spence) and one can't help but feel that Stan Lee and Bill Everett may have taken some inspiration for Marvel's Daredevil from the same source.

The "wandering swordsman with child in tow" is also reminiscent of the *Lone Wolf and Cub* series of Samurai films (1972-74), though the extravagant bloodletting in those films would be at odds with the restraint of *Blind Fury*.

Hauer's star shone brightly, if relatively briefly, during the '80s, and he seemed unable to get out of the shadow of his two most famous screen incarnations - as the homicidal replicant Roy Batty in Ridley Scott's *Blade Runner* (1982) and the mysterious, psychotic, title character of *The Hitcher* (1986). After working with fellow countryman Paul Verhoeven in his native Holland on such films as *Soldier of Orange* (1977) and *Spetters* (1980), he made his Hollywood debut as the villainous Wulfgar in the Stallone action thriller

Nighthawks (1981) before working with Scott and, soon after, with Sam Peckinpah on the director's final film *The Osterman Weekend* (1983). He continued to work consistently and well, becoming a cult figure in cinema (*Salute of the Jugger* [1989], *Wedlock* [1993], and *The Sisters Brothers* [2018]).

His performance in *Blind Fury* is wonderful - those startling eyes have rarely been used to better effect. It may have been a conscious attempt to soften his image, but Roy and the Hitcher still loomed too large.

Australian-born director Noyce came to prominence with the psycho-thriller *Dead Calm* (1989), starring Sam Neill, Nicole Kidman and Billy Zane. Something of a "safe pair of hands" as a director, his other credits include *Patriot Games* (1992), starring Harrison Ford, *Sliver* (1993) starring Sharon Stone, *Clear and Present Danger* (1994) with Ford again and *The Giver* (2014), based on Lois Lowry's award-winning novel.

There's nothing too flashy here, apart from a moment of slow motion that is more Kurosawa than Peckinpah. The camera moves when it needs to, and there is an economy of setup and storytelling that packs a lot into a relatively short running time.

The film's title sequence, for example, serves as a prologue, delivering Nick's backstory, and its singular flashback underscores one of the few introspective moments when Nick forgives Frank for abandoning him in Vietnam. It's a corny moment, but an effective one.

Terry O'Quinn is probably best known for *The Stepfather* (1987) and its sequel *Stepfather II* (1989) and as the mysterious John Locke in *Lost* (2004-2010). Lisa Blount also appeared in *An Officer and a Gentleman* (1982) and *Prince of Darkness* (1987). Noble Willingham as MacCready gives a beautifully clichéd good ol' boy performance, broad when it needs to be, narrow and icy at other times. He enjoyed a long career in film in television including *The Last Picture Show* (1971) and *Paper Moon* (1973). *Blind Fury* was Call's first major screen appearance and, as Billy, he tugs at the heartstrings.

Some films aspire to be art, others are content to be entertainment.

The vast majority fall somewhere in-between.

If *Blind Fury* is content to be entertainment, it is nevertheless quality entertainment.

And quality nonsense.

The Dollmaker

by Rachel Bellwoar

For a TV movie, Daniel Petrie's *The Dollmaker* is on the long side (or maybe it just seems that way in 2023), but when it first aired on Mother's Day on ABC in 1984 there would've been no way to pause it. Two and half hours is fairly normal for a feature length movie but add in commercials and that's a significant chunk of time to commit. Not the best conditions for watching a movie in the era of streaming, yet *The Dollmaker* is one of those rare films that warrants being two and half hours long, and when you look at the source material it shouldn't come as a surprise (my copy of the book reaches 677 pages).

Released in 1954, Harriette Arnow's novel 'The Dollmaker' is about a family who end up moving to Detroit for work. It's WWII, and not only are factory jobs supposed to be patriotic, they're supposed to offer better pay. For most of this adaptation, future husband and wife team Susan Cooper and Hume Cronyn stay pretty close to Arnow's original text. Before this teleplay, Cooper had written a few episodes for British children's television shows (she is also a children's book author) while Cronyn was probably best known as an actor (his villainous turn in *Brute Force* being a highlight). The biggest changes to the

film come at the end and with the characterization of the main character Gertie (played by Jane Fonda).

In her memoir 'My Life So Far', Fonda described Gertie as one of her favorite roles, one she and executive producer Bruce Gilbert had been trying to get off the ground for years before filming actually started. Fonda was already trying to improve her whittling skills while filming *9 to 5* and when filming was over she would join Dolly Parton on a tour bus in Tennessee to meet the people who lived in the surrounding mountains.

The Dollmaker is actually supposed to take place in Kentucky and it opens with a series of still, black-and-white photographs. When Gertie shows up on horseback at the end of the credits, that's when the pictures start moving and the film transitions into color.

The reason Gertie is on horseback is that her youngest son Amos (David Dawson) is sick, and in order to stop a passing car Gertie forces her horse to stand directly in front of it. It's a very telling image - new world vs old world, horse vs. vehicle, with new world trying to bulldoze past but winding up stuck on the side of the road. Wasting no time, Gertie seizes the opportunity to secure her son a ride and, while the military men hold out long enough that Gertie has to perform a tracheotomy on her son (his condition is that bad), she does get her ride in the end.

Most of this opening sequence is in the book, down to Gertie's decision to send her horse home so the army men feel beholden to help her. There is one goof: when Gertie is helping to push the car back onto the road (because no one else is supposed to be around) a man's arm and head can be seen in the background. The film really emphasizes the sign Gertie lays Amos on when she performs the tracheotomy. It's an Uncle Sam poster looking for workers to go to Detroit, and it will foreshadow Gertie's fate (though she doesn't know it yet). The officer (Mike Timoney), who is the main objector to Gertie getting in the car, is definitely softened in the movie. The words are there but it feels like the actor is reluctant to play him as unlikable, where Gertie's an inconvenience to him.

A more important, if subtle, change occurs at the hospital, when Gertie's husband Clovis (Levon Helm) shows up. At its core, *The Dollmaker* is a film about their marriage and their very different views on what success looks like. Gertie wants to save up enough money so they can buy their own farm instead of having to rent and share crops with their landlord. Clovis prefers working with machines and is eager to move to the city to reap the benefits promised by the posters calling for factory workers.

Both think they're doing what's best for their family. Both are so convinced about the righteousness of their plans that they're willing to go behind each other's back to secure them. Clovis has no idea how much money Gertie has saved up in her coat, nor that she plans to buy the Tipton place as soon as he joins the army. Gertie, for her part, has no clue that Clovis doesn't intend to join the army but has actually hidden a suitcase away so that he can sneak off to Detroit under the cover of leaving for his army exam (in the film, we are tipped off to his deception, but in the book readers are caught off guard, like Gertie).

Neither lie is better than the other. They're both really bad, but sheerly due to being a man, Clovis gets his way. Not only is Gertie expected to give up her dream, but the whole town is prepared to enforce her husband's wishes. The Tipton place is suddenly off the market. The unspoken threat is that she won't be allowed to continue renting her house if she tries to ignore Clovis' summons.

Gertie is very much the character that the film and the book sympathizes with, but Clovis isn't a villain which is what makes their conflict fascinating. Yes, Clovis should know Gertie doesn't want to move to Detroit. She's told him so in no uncertain terms. In that sense, he can't claim ignorance, but the trouble with Clovis (and the reason Gertie has resorted to lying) is that Gertie can say how she feels until she's blue in the face. If her wishes contradict Clovis' perception of the world, he simple can't hear them.

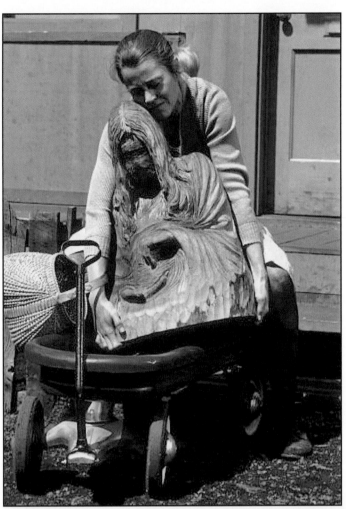

Never mind that Gertie is happy working on the farm. In Clovis' eyes, he has failed her and his family by not being able to provide them with the modern amenities, like electricity, that he covets. To him, Gertie having to work is a travesty. He wants her to not have to worry about farming and to be free to focus on the housework. Clovis fundamentally doesn't understand his wife and while that's not OK, his intentions are good (and also heavily influenced by the perceptions of gender that were prevalent at the time).

Clovis also isn't always wrong (at least not in theory). The schools and ambulances in Detroit might not be as reliable or lifesaving as advertised (as they find out the hard way in the film and book's most memorable scene), but they should be. His loyalty to the union is technically well-placed but his unwillingness to explain why to Gertie is unfair, especially when it coincides with him questioning her intelligence because she's a woman. Instead of being able to come together and resolve their differences, Gertie and Clovis constantly go around each other to try and secure the futures they want for their family. It's a broken marriage, but whereas the film ends on a note of hope, the book doesn't have any to spare.

The differences are subtle at first, like the hospital scene which Amos which I mentioned earlier. In the film, Clovis offers to get Gertie a hamburger and coffee. When she says no, he eventually drops the subject. In the book, Gertie asks Clovis if he can watch Amos so she can get

the coffee herself. All she wants is to step outside and get a drink, but not only does Clovis insist on buying a burger, too, but he doesn't let her get the food herself. It's so hard, because in Clovis' mind he's treating his wife to a meal. He can't comprehend how his actions could be wrong, but to Gertie it's another piece of freedom taken away, and it's only getting worse.

On the surface, these scenes aren't wildly different but these changes build up and, even if the results are the same, they make a difference in terms of Gertie's drive. In the film, Gertie has more opportunities to stand up for herself, like with the Tipton property. In the book, she concedes defeat quickly but in the film she initially tries to fight back even though her efforts are fruitless.

Maybe the book is truer to how a woman in Gertie's position would've behaved in the '40s, whereas Petrie's *The Dollmaker* makes more allowances for how audiences in the '80s would've wanted to see Gertie (and Fonda *as* the character) respond, but that's one of its drawing points: getting to see Fonda's Gertie picking her battles and the toll they take on her.

It's not that Fonda has exclusively played strong characters, but she's someone associated with strength, and it makes the moments when Gertie doesn't speak up all the more painful. Thanks to Fonda, there's never any doubt that Gertie's silence is a choice. Eventually a line will be crossed where she can't hold her tongue, but for now she's biding her time. She's not a passive character, whereas Gertie in the book is more dispirited by the things that happen to her. Both interpretations of the character work, but it's because Gertie gets to tell Clovis off in the film that it's rewatchable. Without such moments, *The Dollmaker* is the sort of film people might admire but only watch once.

STAR WARS
RETURN OF THE JEDI

by James Aaaron

Return of the Jedi debuted to the world an almost unbelievable forty years ago, on May 25, 1983. Though a huge box office success and merchandising juggernaut at the time, it's since been derided by some segments of the fan base and oft described as a puppet-laden kiddie mess overflowing with goofy aliens and too-cute Ewoks. *Jedi* has long been saddled with a poor reputation in comparison to its widely loved predecessors, frequently considered the worst of the original trilogy. Perhaps you've heard: *Return of the Jedi* is the *Godfather III* of blockbuster space operas.

But don't believe everything your friends tell you. As a matter of fact, I come here today to suggest the opposite is true. *Jedi* is not the worst of the trilogy. It's actually my favorite; always has been and always will be.

I freely admit that my opinion is not entirely rooted in the quality of the film itself. My view comes not just from being a lover of the movie, but as a wide-eyed boy who'd turned eight years old a couple of weeks before he first saw it. Forty years ago, and yet I remember that night in so much tiny detail, the way all of us remember the most special moments of our lives. Not in the broad strokes, but in the fine points. Not in the details of the plot, but in the feelings that gripped me as the images flickered before me.

Return of the Jedi was the first movie I ever saw in an actual movie theater. It's the reason I fell in love with cinema, even if I didn't know it at the time. Back then, I was just a kid in a seat, staring at the screen, captured.

I grew up in rural America, in the tiny town of Stanton, Kentucky that lay buried in the Appalachian foothills. We didn't have a proper movie theater but we did have the Mountain View drive-in, and it was usually packed on the weekends well into the 2000s, even after American drive-ins had long since peaked in the '60s.

The Mountain View actually operated as a first-run venue until 2016, when it finally bit the dust thanks not to audience apathy, but the harsh economics of installing new digital projection systems (it still re-opens occasionally for revival viewings of movies like *Grease*). But back in the early '80s, when the drive-in will still showing to capacity crowds every weekend, I took my baby steps into cinema there. I remember those first forays with some fondness, too: *Raiders of the Lost Ark* and *The Fox and the Hound* in 1981, then *E.T. the Extra Terrestrial* the next year. The first movies I ever saw outside of the television. Two Spielberg movies out of the first three, too - not bad. I recall mostly listening to *Raiders*, cowering behind the seat, afraid but also thrilled. *The Fox and the Hound* was blah Disney to me even then, and *E.T.* was exactly what you think it would be to a little boy about the same age as Elliott, the boy on screen - powerful, overwhelming, long-lasting.

Each night when we went to the drive-in, it was the same ritual. Mom parked the car, then we hooked the tinny little speakers to the door frame and waited for the sun to descend enough so that the movie projected clearly against the wooden-plank screens. We usually smuggled our own snacks from home to avoid the costs at the concession stand and also to avoid walking there in the dark. I was the oldest of the three children but I usually sat in the back, and by the time the first movie of the double bill was at its end, we kids were asleep. Then we'd head home.

It was a fine experience. Make no mistake. The fact is, any way you can watch a well-made movie is a fine experience. But the Mountain View was no movie theater. Even though I had not yet visited one myself, I knew they were out there in the world and I knew they were different from the Mountain View. I'm not sure I understood just *how* different. But I knew it was different. And to me at that age, different meant *better*.

I can say that with confidence because I know that on that May weekend in 1983, when I found out were going to the city to watch *Return of the Jedi* in an actual, real-life movie theater, I completely flipped out.

Like most boys my age at that particular moment in history, I was completely obsessed with *Star Wars*. But oddly enough, when I watched *Return of the Jedi*, I had only seen the first movie on TV a handful of times. I had never seen *The Empire Strikes Back;* I actually wasn't even

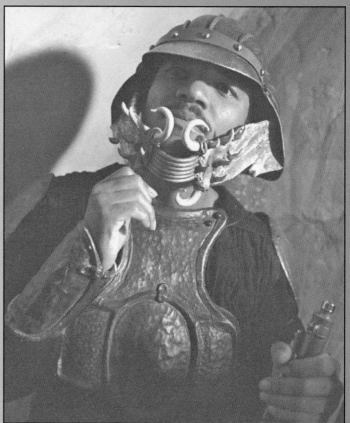

aware that *The Empire Strikes Back* existed! Most of my *Star Wars* love and nearly all my *Star Wars* knowledge came from playing with the toys. I owned several action figures - C-3PO, Luke, Greedo, Ben Kenobi - before having seen even one second of any of the films, and made up my own story about who they were and what they did well before I watched on television for the first time as Luke Skywalker used the Force and flew his X-Wing into the teeth of that Death Star trench (imagine my surprise when I found out Greedo was, in fact, *not* the main villain of the film.) And of course, my friends had other figures, and that was where I learned about Lando Calrissian and Yoda and Boba Fett, although in hindsight, I'm not sure my friends really knew anything about the movie *Empire*, either. We certainly never talked about anything that actually happened in the second movie. We just thought our "Star Wars men" were cool.

By the time *Return of the Jedi* rolled around, I had been playing with the toys and watching *Star Wars* on TV enough to become completely enamored. With the *Jedi* ads saturating the airwaves around me, I was primed and ready.

The little details of that night still live in my mind like all of the other huge moments of my life. I remember all this. We headed toward South Park Cinemas in the larger city of Lexington. It was a forty-five minute drive but in my excitement it seemed ten times that length. As we found a parking space, I could see the crowds already lined up for the next showings, well out the front door and snaking around the side of the building. A theater worker painted a large portrait on the windows surrounding the entranceway, and while I couldn't make much of it out as we drove past or even as I walked by the same window a few minutes later, on the way to buy our tickets, the painter's work would be finished when we came out a few hours later. It turned out to be a giant mock-up of the famous blue *Return of the Jedi* poster, with the hands of a Jedi - presumably Luke Skywalker - arcing his lightsaber into a straight vertical position, the mythical weapon casting its pale glow across a field of stars and planets looming in the background.

I remember all this. We got our tickets and went into the theater. I hadn't seen anything like it before. What looked like three football fields' worth of glass counters and popcorn machines stretched out before me. Posters for coming attractions lined the walls, framed behind glass and ringed by bright light bulbs. The concession stand at the Mountain View Drive-In seemed so small and archaic in comparison, with its single counter and its handful of posters tacked to the wood-panel walls.

We got popcorn and cokes, then made our way back to the theater for our showing. By the time we got in, the previews were over and the movie had actually already started - I missed the opening crawl, which certainly didn't help my confusion about the story. Of course, the place was completely packed, and because there were eight of us - my mother and aunt, my brother and sister, my three cousins, me - there was no way we were going to be able to all sit together. My cousin Khris and I found a couple of open spots in the flickering light, midway towards the screen, near the aisle. There we deposited ourselves. I drank all my coke before the droids got to Jabba the Hutt's desert palace, then fought the urge to go to the bathroom for the last half of the movie. There was no way I was missing anything. I had a Chewbacca figure in my pocket. I remember this.

I sank back into my seat and let *Jedi* overtake me. I truly did not understand most of the story but, really, it didn't matter. Not to me. The magic existed for me in a series of spectacular moments that captured my imagination like nothing really had before. From the arrival of Darth Vader's shuttle on the new Death Star to C-3PO and R2-D2 knocking at the entrance to Jabba's lair to the heroes' Endor celebration following their final vanquish of the evil Empire, each piece of action rolled by almost separate from the others, as if the movie were put together like a giant, moving collage, like a whole much greater than the sum of its parts.

I had very little idea of what was actually going on and it didn't make any difference in the slightest. I loved it. Who is this Jabba the Hutt? Where did he come from? It didn't matter. Why is Han Solo frozen? What is Lando doing here and why is he wearing that funky helmet with teeth? Wait, Boba Fett is dead that quickly? I have his Underoos!

Now Yoda is dying? Wait, there is an actual person under that black helmet? I thought he was a robot! And what is all this about Vader being Luke's dad?

Upon its release, reviews for *Return of the Jedi* were solid, in many cases spectacular. Pre-eminent American critics Roger Ebert and Gene Siskel both gave the movie 4 out of 4 stars. Gerald Clarke in 'Time' said it was "better and more satisfying than *The Empire Strikes Back*." (Though still a huge hit, the comparatively less successful *Empire* had not yet fully gathered the high status it enjoys today). Yet over time, popular perception has settled *Jedi* into a consistent third-place standing among the original *Star*

Wars trilogy. That seems to have translated into it being considered a lesser movie than its two predecessors, when in reality, *Jedi* is right there with them. It's the third movie in terms of chronology, not quality.

Why?

Set aside my own emotional connections. *Jedi* boasts some of the most satisfying action set-pieces not just of the original trilogy but in the entirety of the *Star Wars* franchise. Start with Luke's fight against the Rancor monster, then go straight to the duel at the Sarlacc pit, where Luke takes on Jabba's guards while Princess Leia takes on Jabba himself. From there, we get the speeder bike chase through the redwood forests of Endor. The movie (and the trilogy) caps off with the magnificently intercut trifecta of the Luke-Vader showdown in the Emperor's throne room, the rollicking space battle where Admiral Ackbar leads the rebel fleet against the Empire's horde of cruisers and TIE fighters while General Lando flies the Millenium Falcon into the heart of the Death Star, and the fight on the forest moon of Endor with stormtroopers and two-legged AT-ST walkers slugging it out against Han Solo, Chewbacca, Leia and (yes) those pesky rock-wielding Ewoks.

These are iconic sequences, and with Industrial Light & Magic at the top of its special-effects game, the *Jedi* action bursts off the screen with an artistry that's a notch or two above the previous two films. The spaceship battle around the Death Star is a particular achievement, chock full of TIE fighters, X-wings, B-Wings, A-wings, Y-wings and all

kinds of other fascinating craft swooping through the frame, firing lasers of different colors and blowing each other all to hell. As a child, I clapped and cheered with every action beat, and nearly jumped to my feet when the Falcon outraced the fiery explosion after Lando struck the final blow against the Death Star. As sheer space spectacle, the climatic one in *Return of the* Jedi blew away everything before it, even the trench run in the original *Star Wars*. It remained unmatched for sheer volume of excitement until *Rogue One* more than thirty years later.

Jedi isn't all action, though. The emotion is also there. Luke loses Yoda early in the film, in a beautiful scene where the wise old master takes his "forever sleep" and becomes one with the Force. Still, he leaves young Luke with one last gift - the suggestion (later confirmed by Obi-Wan) that Leia is Luke's sister. Following that, the film and trilogy hurtles towards what I'd consider the single definitive moment in all of *Star Wars*: the Death Star duel between Luke and Darth Vader. Here, Luke finally defeats his personal dark side in a glorious clash of lightsabers whirring among the darkness of the Death Star shadows, while his father Vader gains his redemption in the eyes of his son. A rousing and satisfying conclusion to their story, indeed.

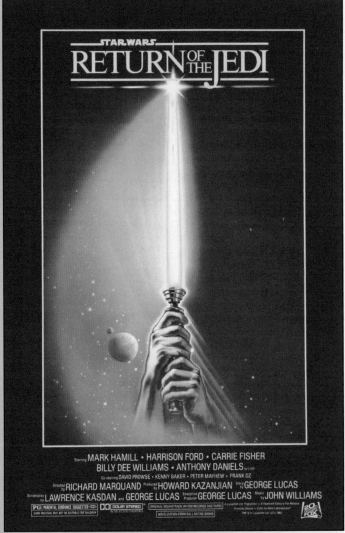

With all this going for it, what drives *Return of the Jedi's* reputation as the worst of the first three movies? Is it really the Ewoks? Here again, I turn to my eight-year-old self and am reminded of what George Lucas said many times during the making of his prequel trilogy: these movies were made for kids. The Ewoks exemplify that as much as anything, and let me tell you, I thought the little creatures were great. I cheered as much for them as I did for Luke, Han and Leia. Even in my young brain I understood the message about their primitive methods overcoming the Empire's technological superiority. More importantly, they were *fun*, and it was *fun* for a kid to see those little creatures with their rocks and handmade bows and sticks-and-animal-skin gliders take down the big bad stormtroopers and all their fancy weaponry. I've never understood the hate.

"I've never understood the hate" is something I could say definitely about *Return of the Jedi* in general. It stands tall with the rest of the series. It captured my imagination in the late spring of 1983 and forever hooked me on a lifetime of movie-going, and it's only gotten better with age. If you haven't seen it in a while, watch it again with fresh eyes and see for yourself.

CLOSING CREDITS

James Aaron

James is an American writer and film lover living in Kentucky with his wife and two dogs. He is the author (as Aaron Saylor) of three novels, including 'Sewerville' and 'Adventures in Terror', the latter of which is set during the horror movie and video store boom of the 1980s.

Rachel Bellwoar

Rachel is a writer for 'Comicon', 'Diabolique' magazine and 'Flickering Myth'. If she could have any director fim a biopic about her life it would be Aki Kaurismäki.

Michael Campochiaro

Michael is a writer, artist and film and pop culture critic living with his family in New York's Hudson Valley. He has been published in the book 'A Very Special Episode, Volume 1: 1957-1985', in which he wrote about *Taxi* and *WKRP In Cincinnati*. He has written for 'Diabolique Magazine', 'Drive-In Asylum', 'HiLoBrow', 'Grumpire' and more. He is also the biggest Michelle Pfeiffer fan you're likely to meet, so reciting lines from *Grease 2*, *Batman Returns* or other Pfeiffer films is a guaranteed way to earn his loyal friendship.

David Flack

David was born and bred in Cambridge. Relatively new to the writing game, he has had reviews published in 'We Belong Dead' and 'Cinema of the '70s'. He loves watching, talking, reading and writing about film and participating on film forums. The best film he has seen in over 55 years of watching is *Jaws* (1975). The worst is *The Creeping Terror* (1963) or anything by Andy Milligan.

Bryan C. Kuriawa

Based in New Jersey, Bryan has spent many years diving into the world of movies. Introduced to the Three Stooges by his grandfather and Japanese cinema when he was eight, he's wandered on his own path, ignoring popular opinions. Willing to discuss and defend everything from Jesus Franco's surreal outings to the 007 masterpiece *Moonraker*, nothing is off-limits. Some of his favorite filmmakers include Ishiro Honda, Jacques Tati, Lewis Gilbert, Jesus Franco and Jun Fukuda.

Simon J. Ballard

Simon lives in Oxford and works in its oldest building, a Saxon Tower. Whilst also working in the adjoining church, he has never felt tempted to re-enact scenes from *Taste the Blood of Dracula* or *Dracula A.D.1972*. He has never done this. Ever. He regularly contributes to the magazine 'We Belong Dead' and its various publications, and once read Edgar Allan Poe's 'The Black Cat' to a garden full of drunk young people at his local gay pub The Jolly Farmers. His first published work was a Top Tip in 'Viz' of which he is justifiably proud.

David Michael Brown

David is a British ex-pat living in Sydney. Working as a freelance writer he has contributed to 'The Big Issue', 'TV Week', 'GQ', 'Rolling Stone' and 'Empire Magazine Australia', where he was Senior Editor for almost eight years. He is presently writing a book on the film music of German electronic music pioneers Tangerine Dream and researching the work of Andy Warhol associate and indie filmmaker Paul Morrissey for a forthcoming project.

Jonathon Dabell

Jonathon was born in Nottingham in 1976. He is a huge film fan and considers '70s cinema his favourite decade. He has written for 'Cinema Retro' and 'We Belong Dead', and co-authored 'More Than a Psycho: The Complete Films of Anthony Perkins' and 'Ultimate Warrior: The Complete Films of Yul Brynner' with his wife. He lives in Yorkshire with his wife, three kids, three cats and two rabbits!

John Harrison

John is a Melbourne, Australia-based freelance writer and film historian who has written for numerous genre publications, including 'Fatal Visions', 'Cult Movies', 'Is It Uncut?', 'Monster!' and 'Weng's Chop'. Harrison is also the author of the Headpress book 'Hip Pocket Sleaze: The Lurid World of Vintage Adult Paperbacks', has recorded audio commentaries for Kino Lorber, and composed the booklet essays for the Australian Blu-ray releases of *Thirst*, *Dead Kids* and *The Survivor*. 'Wildcat!', Harrison's book on the film and television career of former child evangelist Marjoe Gortner, was published by Bear Manor in 2020.

James Lecky

James is an actor, writer and occasional stand-up comedian who has had a lifelong obsession with cinema, beginning with his first visit to the Palace Cinema in Derry, (now long since gone) to see *Chitty Chitty Bang Bang* when he was six. Since then, he has happily wallowed in cinema of all kinds but has a particular fondness for Hammer movies, spaghetti westerns, Euro-crime and samurai films.

Kevin Nickelson

Kevin has been a fan of cinema of all genres and decades since age 4. As he grew older he found his passions for dissecting various aspects of film and decided to marry this obsession with his ability for creative writing into writing about film. Kevin has written for 'Scarlet the Magazine', the 'Van Helsing Confidential' and the site classic-horror.com. Currently, he writes for 'We Belong Dead' magazine and books, 'Scary Monsters' magazine, horrornews.net and will soon be working for 'Scream' magazine. Kevin is also co-host of the Grim and Bloody podcast produced by Death's

Joseph Secrett

Joseph is a film nut and collector who started at a young age, and quickly became infatuated with all things cinematic. He is a huge fan of 20th century cinema, especially the '60s and '70s for their sheer diversity of genres. Top choices of his include revisionist westerns and seedy crime dramas.

Ian Talbot Taylor

After early short story successes, Ian began editing music fanzines and spent decades acting, directing and adjudicating in amateur theatre for the Greater Manchester Drama Federation. He writes for 'The Dark Side', 'Infinity', 'Scream', 'Fantastic Fifties', 'Halls of Horror' and 'We Belong Dead' (and is on the editorial team of the latter). His book on the films of Jenny Agutter appeared in 2021. Ian has progressed from 'prose dabbler' to prolific fiction writer, contributing to and co-editing the BHF Books of Horror. He recently released the collaborative fiction collection 'Spoken in Whispers' and also presents shows for Radio M29 .

Darren Linder

Darren grew up in the '70s and has been forever enamored with films from that decade. He is a lifelong resident of Oregon, currently living in Portland. He has performed in many rock bands, ran a non-profit dog rescue, and worked in social service with at-risk youths. His favorite film directors of the '80s are John Carpenter, Brian De Palma and James Cameron.

Peter Sawford

Peter was born in Essex in 1964 so considers himself a child of the '70s. A self-confessed film buff, he loves watching, reading about and talking about cinema. A frustrated writer his whole life, he's only recently started submitting what he writes to magazines. His favourite director is Alfred Hitchcock with Billy Wilder running him a close second. He still lives in Essex with his wife and works as an IT trainer and when not watching films he's normally panicking over who West Ham are playing next.

Aaron Stielstra

Aaron was born in Ann Arbor, Michigan and grew up in Tucson, AZ and NYC. He is an actor, writer, director, soundtrack composer and illustrator. Since moving to Italy in 2012, he has appeared in spaghetti westerns, numerous crime movies, and horror-thrillers - most of them very wet - and recently completed the punk-rock comedies Weber Falls, USA and Excretion: the Shocking True Story of the Football Mom. He can be seen performing in his band War, Covid & Trump. His favorite '80s actor is Willem Dafoe.

Dr. Andrew C. Webber

Dr. W, a film teacher and examiner for over 35 years, already writes passionately for 'Cinema of the '70s' magazine and also contributes to the cassette gazette fanzine. He pontificates about music on the Low Noise podcast (available on Apple and Spotify) and his blogs can occasionally be found on Oxford's Ultimate Picture Palace cinema website. He still loves being "at" the movies and would describe himself as a lover of cinema, if asked.